EARLY AMERICAN PORTRAIT DRAUGHTSMEN IN CRAYONS

Library of American Art

EARLY AMERICAN PORTRAIT DRAUGHTSMEN IN CRAYONS

By Theodore Bolton

Kennedy Graphics, Inc. • Da Capo Press
New York • 1970

This edition of
Early American Portrait Draughtsmen in Crayons
is an unabridged republication of the
first edition published in New York in 1923.

Library of Congress Catalog Card Number 74-77724

SBN 306-71362-4

Copyright 1923 by Frederic Fairchild Sherman

Published by Da Capo Press
A Division of Plenum Publishing Corporation
227 West 17th Street, New York, N.Y. 10011

EARLY AMERICAN
PORTRAIT DRAUGHTSMEN
IN CRAYONS

SAINT-MÉMIN: MRS. JOHN COX
Property of the Misses Smith

EARLY AMERICAN PORTRAIT
DRAUGHTSMEN IN CRAYONS

BY
THEODORE BOLTON

NEW YORK
FREDERIC FAIRCHILD SHERMAN
MCMXXIII

LIST OF ILLUSTRATIONS

To

JESSE LEE BENNETT

THE present volume lists as much of the work by portrait draughtsmen in crayons, both native Americans and foreign artists working in America, from the earliest times until 1860 as has come to the notice of the author.

It includes portraits drawn in black crayon, colored crayons or pastels and black lead pencil. Several outline portraits in ink are listed. It is a companion volume to "Early American Portrait Painters in Miniature."

FOREWORD

I

The word "crayon" is derived from the Latin "creta"
meaning chalk. A crayon is chalk in some form con-
venient for drawing. Black crayon is generally enclosed
in wood or in spiral wrappings of paper.

A pastel is a colored crayon. The word "pastel" is
derived from the Latin "pastillus" meaning a small roll
or lozenge. It is generally protected by a sheath of paper which is trimmed off as the color is used up. The
process of drawing in pastels is identical with any other
drawing process except that the surface drawn upon is
generally coarser than ordinary drawing paper and has
what is called a "tooth." Rough paper, sand paper, canvas and even chamois are used as drawing surfaces.

Perhaps the earliest important portrait drawings in
colored crayons are those by the Clouet family of artists
portraying personages at the court of Francis the First.
These are usually in two colors — in black outline with
the lips, ears and corners of the eyes drawn in red.
Sometimes the cheeks are modelled in "sanguine." Probably inspired by their example Hans Holbein about this
time enhanced his silver point portraits with one or more
colors, a method he carried to perfection in his English
portraits drawn at the court of Henry the Eighth. Ti-
moteo Viti in Italy also drew a few portraits in several
colors.

These portraits however should properly be called colored drawings. The pastel portrait generally spoken of is one in which all the colors are employed and the drawing surface is practically covered. In this sense Maurice Quentin Latour, Jean Baptiste Chardin, Jean Baptiste Greuze and Jean Etienne Liotard were among the most eminent pastel portrait draughtsmen of Continental Europe in the eighteenth century.

During the previous century England produced a number of excellent portrait draughtsmen in pastel. The half dozen or more pastels now remaining by Edmund Ashfield rank him as one of the masters in the art. Many of his portraits probably perished during the civil wars. John Russell was one of the outstanding English pastellists of the eighteenth century.

Sweden produced at least one master in Lundberg who died about 1780. The same century and later there were a number of excellent Irish pastellists.

More fragile even than miniatures, pastel portraits can be ruined by jolting which dislodges the particles of color or by a touch which will remove the crayon dust completely. A spray of shellac called "fixitif" helps to settle the crayon more permanently to the paper or canvas but at the risk of losing the color. To guard the pastel portrait it is usually framed with glass which, moreover, must not touch the surface of the drawing.

The word "pencil" is derived from the Latin "penicillum" meaning brush. A pencil is a sharply pointed brush. In the more frequent and modern sense a pencil is a thin rod of plumbago or graphite encased in wood which is sharpened to expose a point of the carbon. It is often called a "black lead pencil" or "lead pencil." The term "black lead" is a misnomer arising from the fact that drawings made with lead are of a silvery quality and drawings made in graphite, which is pure carbon, are a deep black. The term "black lead" still persists however as good usage in spite of the fact that the cause for this distinction has long ceased to exist.

II

The pastel portrait in English colonial America was never so popular as the portrait in oil or miniature. Perhaps the nature of the medium requiring glass for its protection made it less in demand.

John Singleton Copley was the first important American portrait draughtsman in pastel. Blackburn who came to Boston about 1754, made a few pastel portraits on canvas which may have influenced Copley.

John Johnston made a number of pastel portraits in Boston, among them one of himself. Somewhat earlier Benjamin Blyth worked extensively at Salem. John Hazlitt made at least one pastel portrait at Hingham. The great miniature painter Edward Malbone also made one and possibly more.

The most important pastellist during the first two decades of the Republic was undoubtedly the prolific worker James Sharples, an Englishman who worked extensively in the United States and died here. Sharples was educated in France and although it is not at all certain that he received any artistic instruction in that country it is evident that his excellent small profiles in colored chalks were inspired by the French artists who made profile drawings for engravers.

Gradually the colored chalk of the pastellists gave way to the black chalk of the crayon portrait draughtsmen. The greatest of these was the Frenchman, Charles Balthazer Julien Fevret de Saint-Mémin. For each of the seven hundred and fifty or more portrait engravings that he produced there was always a life size crayon drawing and many of these still exist. Nearly all of his portraits were made in the United States and he worked almost the same period as Sharples.

In John Vanderlyn's excellent black crayon portraits made for the most part during the first years of the nineteenth century there is again a French influence. Unfortunately the artist drew but a few of these as his time was largely taken up with historical compositions.

Impetus to the art was given by Edward Miles, the English miniature painter who settled in Philadelphia. There were a number of "pupils of Mr. Miles." In Philadelphia too lived James Barton Longacre who drew many small pencil portraits — often from life, sometimes from other portraits — and after these he made engravings for his monumental "National Portrait Gallery." His associate in this undertaking, James Herring, likewise made small pencil portraits.

The portrait drawings of the eminent painter, Thomas Sully, were used almost exclusively as studies for his portraits in oils. He, however, also made a few pastels in color.

During the eighteen forties many portrait draughtsmen in black crayon appeared. Among these were Seth Cheney and Savinien Dubourjal, who both received training in France. Seth Cheney in his day was ranked highly.

The following decade produced many more artists in crayon. Besides those who exist merely as names in old city directories were George Lambdin and Alexander

Lawrie. The popular English pencil portrait draughtsman, Samuel Lawrence, came to the country for a year in 1854.

Two artists who began to work about this time stand prominently above their numerous contemporaries — Eastman Johnson and Samuel W. Rowse. Both outlived the century. Johnson started making crayon portraits in 1841 and continued to do so the rest of his life although he was primarily a painter. His friend Rowse started about 1851 and remained a portrait draughtsman in crayons exclusively save for a very few portraits in oils.

The decline of the crayon portrait came a little later than that in the case of the portrait in miniature. Both had to compete with the photograph but whereas the art of miniature painting declined quickly, the art of the crayon was for years extensively used to retouch enlarged photographs. Although innumerable portraits were made in this manner, these have neither an artistic nor documentary value and have generally met deserved destruction in the trash heap. The year 1860 may be stated as the approximate date of the decadence. A few men like Rowse still kept up a high average but the best days of the crayon portrait had already passed into history.

III

I wish to thank all those who in various ways have helped me in the present undertaking.

The assistance given me by Mr. Harry MacNeill Bland of New York calls for my especial thanks. He has not only looked over my manuscript but has given me much information as well.

Mr. David C. Mearns of Washington, D. C., has also supplied me with information for which I wish to thank him publicly.

As in the case of my previous volume "Early American Portrait Painters in Miniature," I am chiefly indebted to Mr. Ruel Pardee Tolman and Mr. Frederic Fairchild Sherman. To Mr. Tolman I am indebted, in this instance, for taking charge of my notes during my frequent trips away from Washington. To Mr. Sherman I am indebted for his care in the press work of the book as well as for assistance during its writing.

THEODORE BOLTON

Washington, D. C., October, 1922.

AKERS, Charles

b. *October 5, 1836, Maine; living in New York in 1879.*
Sculptor and crayon portrait draughtsman.

He worked in New York and during 1860, 1869, and 1875 had a studio in Waterbury, Connecticut.

ALEXANDER, Francis

b. *February 3, 1800, Killingsby, Connecticut; d. 1880, Florence, Italy.*
Portrait Painter.

Alexander wrote a short autobiography published in Dunlap's "History." He went to New York for a brief period in 1820 and again the following year for study under Alexander Robertson. He then went to Boston with a letter to Gilbert Stuart from John Trumbull where he advanced rapidly in his painting under Stuart's influence. In 1831 he first visited Italy. He did not in his final years continue his profession as an artist. He drew on stone the earliest attempts at portrait lithography in America. For full account see Boston Magazine, 1825.

1. Longfellow, Henry Wadsworth. (1807-1882.) Drawn 1852. Pastel. Reproduced in S. Longfellow: Life of Longfellow, v. 2.

ALLEN, Sarah Lockhart

b. *August 2, 1793, Salem, Massachusetts; d. there July 11, 1877.*
Miniature painter and pastel portrait draughtsman.

In Felt's "Annals of Salem" there is the following note under the year 1820: "Portraits of full size are executed by Miss Sarah Allen in crayons. She is a native of this city." All the above information was furnished the writer by Mr. Henry W. Belknap of Salem.

ANDERSON, ALEXANDER

b. *April 21, 1775, New York City; d. April 18, 1870, Jersey City.*

Engraver upon copper and wood.

Graduated from the Medical Department of Columbia University in 1796. He had previously engraved on copper and resumed engraving in 1797 and 1798 permanently gave up medicine for engraving. In 1820 he became interested in wood engraving and developed the art in America to such an extent that he is known as the Father of Wood Engraving in the United States. See Stauffer; American Engravers. He made many pencil and wash drawings.

    1. Anderson, John. Etched by Albert Rosenthal after a drawing by Alexander Anderson. Published by Dodd, Mead and Company.

ANDRÉ, JOHN

b. *1751, London; d. October 2, 1780, Tappan on the Hudson.*

British army officer and amateur artist.

Major André who was executed as a spy during the American Revolution was an amateur artist of great ability. He painted water color landscapes;

Anderson — André: 3

COLONEL SAMUEL FLAGG
BY JOHN JOHNSTON
Property of Mrs. Richard Greene

assisted at the festivals given in Philadelphia by designing costumes for the "Mischianza" pageants; possibly carved the wooden figure of a dragoon in the Wister House in Germantown; and undoubtedly designed scenery for a small theater in Southwark. He also drew small portraits in pencil and painted a few miniatures. His own account with sketches of the "Mischianza" festival is published in the "Century Magazine," March, 1894. He cut a series of silhouettes of Washington, Franklin, etc., owned by Mr. Robert Fridenberg of New York.

1. Shippen, Miss Peggy. (1761-1804.) Pencil. Owned by the Historical Society of Pennsylvania. Reproduced in T. Bolton: Early American Portrait Painters in Miniature.

ARMSTRONG, William G.

b. *1823, Montgomery Co., Pa.; living in Philadelphia, 1880.*

Engraver, portrait painter in water color and portrait draughtsman.

Armstrong was a pupil of Longacre in Philadelphia, drew small portraits and finally became a line engraver. He engraved several portraits for Longacre's "National Portrait Gallery."

1. Barney, Joshua. (1759-1818.) "Engraved by J. Gross from a drawing by W. G. Armstrong after a miniature by "Isabey."
2. Laurens, Henry. (1724-1792.) "Engraved by T. B. Welch from a drawing by W. G. Armstrong after the portrait by J. S. Copley."
3. Sumter, Major General Thomas. (1736-1832.) "Engraved by G. Parker from a drawing by W. G. Armstrong after the original Portrait by C. W. Peale."

Armstrong: 4

AUDUBON, John James

b. *April 26, 1785, Haiti, West Indies;* d. *Jan. 27, 1851, New York City.*
Ornithologist and artist.

The celebrated ornithologist Audubon was the son of Captain Jean Audubon and a Creole woman named Rabin. He was legally adopted in France by both his father and his father's legal wife, Anne Moynet Audubon. He was in America from 1804 to 1805 visiting France in 1806. It was probably at this time that he received the instruction in drawing from Louis David of which he speaks in his "Journal." In 1807 he returned to America. He travelled extensively in the United States and Canada, making notes and drawings for his "Birds of North America" and "Quadrupeds of North America." He was in England and Scotland from 1826 to 1830. He revisited England in 1837 and lived there until 1839. See F. H. Herrick: "Audubon, the Naturalist." See also "Scribner's," March, 1893.

1. Benedict, Jennett, later Mrs. Butts. Black crayon. 14½ x 10½. Signed: "J. J. Audubon 1824." Owned by Mr. F. Sterling, Cleveland, Ohio. Reproduced in F. H. Herrick: Audubon, the Naturalist, v. 1, p. 342.
2. Symmes, John Cleves. (1742-1814.) Pencil. Owned by the New York Historical Society.
3. Lafayette, Marquis de. (1757-1834.) Crayon. Drawn from life at New Orleans in 1825.

BADGER, John C.

Flourished 1855, Philadelphia.
Crayon portrait draughtsman.

Audubon — Badger: 5

He exhibited at the Pennsylvania Academy. He must not be confused with Joseph W. Badger who painted miniatures in New York from 1832 to 1838, nor with the two artists who painted portraits in Boston: Thomas Badger lived there from 1836 to 1859 and James W. Badger lived there from 1845 to 1846.

BARRY, CHARLES A.

Flourished 1851-1859, Boston.
Portrait painter and portrait draughtsman in crayons.
  1. Lincoln, Abraham.

BENSELL, G. F.

Flourished 1855-1868, Philadelphia.
Portrait draughtsman in crayons.

BIRCH, B.

Flourished 1784.
Portrait draughtsman in crayons, seal engraver and watch maker.

Inserted an advertisement in the N. Y. Packet, Nov. 25, 1784. See W. Kelby: Notes on American Artists.

BIRCH, WILLIAM RUSSELL

b. *April 9, 1755, Warwick, England;* d. *August 7, 1834, Philadelphia.*
Miniature painter in enamel, etcher and engraver.

Exhibited forty-one miniatures at the Royal Academy during 1781 and 1782. Sir Joshua Reynolds employed him to make miniature copies of his

Barry — Birch: 6

portraits. In 1794 he settled in Philadelphia. Extracts from an unpublished autobiography of William Birch are published in Anne Hollingsworth Wharton's Heirlooms in Miniatures. See also T. Bolton: Early American Portrait Painters in Miniature, where twenty of his miniatures are listed.

1-2. Two portraits of unidentified sitters. Drawings owned by Mr. Albert Rosenthal, Philadelphia, 1922.

BLACK, WILLIAM THURSTON

Flourished 1850-1851, Philadelphia and New York.
Portrait painter and portrait draughtsman in pastel and crayon.

BLACKBURN, JOSEPH

Flourished 1753-1716, Bermuda and Boston.
Portrait painter in oils and portrait draughtsman in pastel.

Mr. John Hill Morgan in the Brooklyn Museum "Quarterly" for January, July and October, 1919, established the fact that this artist's name was Joseph Blackburn and not, as is frequently written Jonathan B. Blackburn. He probably came from England. He is first heard of in Bermuda where he came in 1753 to paint portraits of several members of the Tucker family. This information is given in T. A. Emmett's "Tucker Family in Bermuda," New York, 1893, where several of the Tucker portraits are reproduced. From 1754 to 1761 he was painting portraits in Boston. He may have visited Portsmouth as many of his sitters came from that city.

Black — Blackburn: 7

1. Deering, Thomas. (1720-1785.) 22⅛ x 17¾. Pastel on canvas, Metropolitan Museum.

BLYTH, BENJAMIN

b. *1746, Salem, Massachusetts;* d. *after 1787.*
Portrait draughtsman in pastel.

The son of Samuel Blyth. He was admitted to the Essex Lodge of Masons in Salem on March 1, 1781. In Felt's "Annals of Salem" under the date 1769, there is the following entry: "Benjamin Blyth draws crayons at his father's house in the great street leading to Marblehead. He painted with great success in colored crayons. Many of his portraits are extant in the ancient families of this city. The writer recollects to have seen a production of this kind from his hand which represented the celebrated Whitefield in the attitude of preaching."

1. Adams, John. (1735-1826.) Owned by Mrs. Charles Francis Adams. Reproduced in C. W. Bowen: Centennial of Inauguration of Washington.
2. Adams, Mrs. John, née Abigail Smith. Formerly owned by C. F. Adams.
3. Curwen, Judge Samuel. (1715-1802.) Drawn 1772. Essex Institute.
4. Curwen, Sarah. (1742-1775.) Drawn 1772. Essex Institute.
5. Gibaut, John. (1767-1805.) Attributed to Blyth. Essex Institute.
6. Holyoke, Dr. Edward. (1689-1769.)
7. Stone, Elizabeth, later Mrs. Captain White. Essex Institute.
8. Thomas, General. Drawn 1777. Owned in Yonkers, New York.

Blyth: 8

9. Washington, George. After C. W. Peale. Engraved by
J. Norman. See Hart: Engraved Portraits of Washington, No. 43.
10. White, Captain Joseph. (1748-1803. Essex Institute.
11. Whitefield, Reverend George. (1714-1770.)

BOUDIER

Flourished early nineteenth century.
Engraver and crayon portrait draughtsman.

According to Bayley and Goodspeed, Boudier
"was an engraver of portrait plates in the style of
St. Memin; probably a visitor making a brief stay
in this country, only one engraving with his signature being known." For his plates he must have
made crayon portraits. The engraving mentioned
is of Napoleon, Stauffer, No. 209.

BOWERS, EDWARD

Flourished 1855-1858, Philadelphia.
Portrait painter in oils and crayon portrait draughts-
man.

BROWN, "MYSTERIOUS"

Flourished 1812, New York City.
Miniature painter and crayon portrait draughtsman.

BROWN was an Englishman who came to New
York and stayed several years. He gave much as-
sistance to Nathaniel Rogers the miniature painter.
See Dunlap: "History of the Arts of Design."

BROWERE, JOHN HENRI ISAAC

b. *November 18, 1792, New York City;* d. *there Sep-*
tember 10, 1834.
Sculptor of life masks.

Boudier — Browere: 9

He made life masks of Thomas Jefferson, Gilbert Stuart, the captors of John André and many other eminent Americans. See Charles Henry Hart: Life Masks of Eminent Americans, a most important historical book well illustrated.

1. Anderson, Alexander. (1775-1870.) The wood engraver. Inscribed: "A. Anderson Act at 44. Drawn by Browere." Reproduced in wood cut by T. Sudgen. Owner of wood cut Mr. Harry MacNeill, Bland, N. Y.

CHENEY, SETH WELLS

b. Nov. 28, 1810, East Hartford, Connecticut; d. September 10, 1856, South Manchester, Connecticut. Engraver and crayon portrait draughtsman.

SETH WELLS CHENEY, the brother of John Cheney the engraver, studied in Boston in 1829. In 1833 he went to Paris and studied under Isabey and Delaroche, returning in 1834. He started drawing crayon portraits in Boston in 1841. In 1849 he revisited Europe. See Edna D. Cheney: "Memoir of Seth W. Cheney," Boston, 1881; and also S. R. Koehler: "Catalogue of the work of John Cheney and Seth Wells Cheney," Boston, 1890. His portrait drawings are in black and white crayons. A memorial exhibition of the work of John and Seth Wells Cheney at the Boston Museum in 1893 included 338 engravings, paintings, drawings and two or three objects of sculpture. The catalogue of that display forms the basis of the appended register.

1. Appleton, Harriet S. Owned by Mr. T. J. Coolidge.
2. Appleton, Hetty S. Owned by Mr. T. J. Coolidge.

Cheney: 10

3. Appleton, Mrs. Nathan. Drawn 1846. Owned by Mr. Wm. S. Appleton.
4. Appleton, Mrs. Robert. Owned by Mrs. C. C. Jackson.
5. Appleton, Mrs. William. Drawn 1842. Owned by Mrs. W. C. Loring.
6. Appleton, Mrs. William C. Drawn 1845. Owned by Mr. W. C. Appleton.
7. Appleton, William S. Owned by Mr. W. S. Appleton.
8. Apthorp, William Foster, at the age of 7. Drawn 1854. Owned by Mrs. E. D. Cheney.
9. Barnard, Charles. (b. 1838.) Owned by Mr. J. M. Barnard.
10. Bowditch, Charlotte. Owned by the estate of J. I. Bowditch.
11. Bowditch, Lucy. Owned by the estate of J. I. Bowditch.
12. Brown, Henry K. (1814-1886.) Owned by Mr. H. K. Bush-Brown.
13. Brown, Mrs. Henry K. Owned by Mr. H. K. Bush-Brown.
14. Bryant, William Cullen. (1794-1878.) Drawn 1847. Owned by Parke Goodwin. Engraved by J. Cheney.
15. Cheney, Charles. (1804-1874.) Owned by Mr. F. W. Cheney.
16. Cheney, Mrs. Edna D. Drawn 1854. Unfinished. Owned by Mrs. E. D. Cheney.
17. Cheney, Mrs. Edna D. Drawn 1854. Unfinished. Owned by Mrs. E. D. Cheney. (This portrait is drawn in sanguine.)
18. Cheney, Mrs. Electra Woodbridge. Owned by Mrs. R. Goodman.
19. Cheney, Seth Wells. (1810-1856.) Self portrait. Owned by Mrs. E. A. Goodman.
20. Cheney, Ward. (1813-1876.) Owned by Mrs. A. Cheney.
21. Cheney, Mrs. Ward. Owned by Mrs. J. B. Powell.
22. Clarke, Jane. Drawn 1854. Sketch in sanguine. Owned by Mrs. E. D. Cheney.

Cheney — *Continued:* 11

GENERAL ANTHONY WAYNE
BY JOHN TRUMBULL
Collection of Mr. Charles A. Munn

23. Crafts, Mrs. Mariann M. Owned by Mrs. F. B. Ellison.
24. Cunningham, Mrs. John A., née Alice Haskell. Owned by Mr. J. A. Cunningham.
25. Curtis, Mrs. Charles P., née Margaret Stevenson. Drawn 1846. Owned by Mrs. I. P. Curtis.
26. Dix, Dorothea Lynde. (1794-1887.) Owned by the Boston Athenaeum.
27. Emerson, George Samuel. Owned by Mrs. J. Lowell.
28. Fox, Katy, at 14 years of age. Drawn 1849, New York. Owned by Mrs. R. Goodman.
29. Frothingham, Mrs. S. Owned by Mrs. J. H. Wolcott.
30. Gardiner, George A. Owned by Miss O. E. Gardiner.
31. Goddard, Mrs. Cornelia Amory, later Mrs. C. G. Loring. Drawn 1848. Owned by Miss A. C. Lowell.
32. Goddard, Mrs. C. A., and her son George. Owned by Miss A. C. Lowell.
33. Goodman, Mrs. Richard, née Miss Cheney. Owned by Mrs. R. Goodman.
34. Goodman, Rosalie Cheney. Charcoal. Owned by Mrs. R. Goodman.
35. Goodman, Rosalie Cheney. Drawn 1850.
36. Grant, Elizabeth W. Owned by Mr. P. Grant.
37. Gray, Asa. (1810-1888.)
38. H. This portrait is noted as "H. W. H." Drawn 1842. Owned by Mr. E. H. Halle.
39. Hammond, Samuel. (1757-1842); and Gardiner Greene. Owned by Mr. G. G. Hammond.
40. Hammond, Mrs. Susan Greene. Owned by Mr. C. G. Hammond.
41. Hooper, Mrs. Ann. Unfinished. Owned by Mrs. E. D. Cheney.
42. Howes, Mrs. Frederick. Owned by Mrs. S. B. Cabot.
43. Howes, Lucy Cabot. Owned by Miss E. Howes.
44. Hunt, Eben Lewis. Drawn 1852. Owned by Miss S. H. Hunt.
45. Huntington, Rev. Frederick Daniel. Drawn about 1843. Owned by the sitter.

Cheney — Continued: 12

46. Huntington, Mrs. F. D., née Hannah Dane Sargent. Drawn 1843. Owned by the sitter.

47. Jackson, Dr. Charles T. Owned by Mrs. C. T. Jackson.

48. Jackson, Dr. James. Drawn 1842. Owned by Mrs. A. C. Lowell.

49 Jackson, Dr. James. Owned by Mr. G. G. Hammond.

50. Jackson, Mrs. James, née Sarah Cabot. Owned by Dr. C. P. Putnam.

51. Lang, Mrs. William Bailey. Owned by Mrs. A. Bailey.

52. Lawrence, Mrs. Amos A., at 16 years of age. Drawn 1840-1841. Owned by Mrs. H. L. Hemenway.

53. Lawrence, Mrs. Amos A., née Sarah E. Appleton. Owned by Miss Julia Lawrence.

54. Leslie, Mrs. Susan Lyman. Drawn 1854. Owned by Mrs. E. D. Cheney.

55. Littlehale, Helen P. Drawn 1854. Owned by Miss M. F. Littlehale.

56. Longfellow, Henry Wadsworth. (1807-1882.) Drawn in 1854. Owned by Miss A. M. Longfellow. Reproduced in Longfellow: Works, v. 7.

57. Loring, Anna, at 13 years of age. Owned by Mrs. O. Dresel.

58. Loring, Charles Greeley, at 13 years of age. (1794-1868.) Owned by Mrs. A. Gray.

59. Loring, C. W. Owned by Miss C. P. Loring.

60. Loring, Francis C. Owned by Miss I. E. Loring.

61. Loring, Miss J. L., later Mrs. Asa Gray. Owned by Mrs. C. W. Loring.

62. Lowell, Ann C. Owned by Mrs. A. T. Lyman.

63. Lowell, Augustus, as a child. Owned by Mr. A. Lowell.

64. Lowell, Ella, at 5 years of age. Owned by Mrs. A. T. Lyman.

65. Lowell, James Russell. (1819-1891.)

66. Lyman, Mrs. Charles T. Owned by Mr. P. Grant.

67. Lyman, Arthur T. Owned by Mr. A. T. Lyman.

68. Mann, Mrs. Lydia. Owned by Miss L. M. Favor.

Cheney—*Continued:* 13

69. Mason, Elizabeth R., at 11 years of age, later Mrs. W. C. Cabot. Drawn 1845. Owned by Mr. W. C. Cabot.
70. Mason, Jane. Owned by Mrs. F. E. Oliver.
71. May, Mrs. Mary. Drawn 1852. Owned by Miss E. G. May.
72. Merrow, Mrs. Lead pencil. Owned by Mrs. E. D. Cheney.
73. Mills, Anna Cabot Lowell (Dwight.) Owned by Mr. A. Mills.
74. Mills, Charles James, as a child. Owned by Mr. A. Mills.
75. Morison, Reverend John H. Owned by Mr. A. Mills.
76. Morse, Mrs. Hazen, née Lucy Cary. Owned by Mr. A. C. Morse.
77. Murdoch, Mrs. Joseph. Drawn 1853. Owned by Mr. A. C. Morse.
78. Parker, Theodore. (1810-1860.)
79. Parker, Mrs. Theodore.
80. Parkman, Dr. Samuel. Owned by Mr. H. Parkman.
81. Peabody, Catherine. Owned by Mr. W. C. Loring.
82. Peabody, Ephraim. (1807-1856.) Owned by Mrs. W. C. Loring.
83. Perkins, Charles Callahan. (1823-1886.) Signed and dated 1842. Owned by Mrs. S. P. Cleveland.
84. Perkins, James Henry, at 16 years of age. Owned by Mrs. S. P. Cleveland.
85. Perkins, Mrs. Thomas H., the second. Drawn about 1841. Owned by Mr. T. H. Perkins.
86. Perkins, Mrs. Thomas H., the third. Drawn about 1840. Owned by Mr. T. H. Perkins.
87. Pierce, Mary. Owned by Mrs. Asa Gray.
88. Pitkin, Adelaide. Lead pencil. Drawn 1852. Owned by Mrs. E. Sherman.
89. Pitkin, Emily. Owned by Mrs. E. Sherman.
90. Pratt, Mary. Owned by Mrs. R. T. Paine.
91. Putnam, Reverend George. Drawn 1842. Owned by Mrs. A. C. Lowell.

Cheney—*Continued:* 14

13

92. Putnam, Mrs. George, née Elizabeth Ann Ware. Owned by Miss A. C. Lowell.
93. Putnam, Caroline and Anna E. Drawn 1842. Owned by Miss A. C. Lowell.
94. Putnam, George and Charles. Drawn 1842-3. Owned by Miss A. C. Lowell.
95. Putnam, Miss E. C. Owned by C. P. Putnam.
96. Putnam, Mrs. John Pickering. Owned by Mrs. J. P. Putnam.
97. Ripley, Mrs. Owned by Mrs. E. D. Cheney.
98. Russell, Samuel H. Drawn 1843. Owned by Mrs. E. D. Cheney.
99. Sanderson, Betsey. Owned by Miss A. C. Lowell.
100. Seaver, Miss, later Mrs. Cowing. Drawn 1853. Owned by Mr. W. H. Cowing.
101. Sedgwick, Catherine Maria. (1789-1867.) Owned by Mrs. E. D. Cheney.
102. Simmons, Mrs. William, née Lucia Hammatt. Owned by Miss E. B. Ripley.
103. Smith, Edna D., later Mrs. E. D. Cheney. Drawn 1851. Owned by Mrs. E. D. Cheney.
104. Smith, Mrs. William. Drawn 1845. Owned by Mrs. W. C. Appleton.
105. Sprague, Mrs. F. G., as a child. Owned by Mr. A. Lowell.
106. Ticknor, Mrs. George. Owned by Miss E. Dexter.
107. Twisleton, Mrs. Edward, née Miss Dwight. Drawn 1852-3. Owned by Mrs. W. W. Vaughan.
108. Twisleton, Mrs. Edward, née Miss Dwight. Owned by Mrs. J. E. Cabot.
109. Wales, Mary Ann. Owned by Miss M. A. Wales.
110. Warren, Emily. Drawn 1844. Owned by Mrs. J. A. Beebe.
111. Wesselhoeft, Minna. Owned by Miss Selma Wesselhoeft.
112. Wigglesworth, Mrs. Thomas. Owned by Mr. T. Wigglesworth.
113. Wigglesworth, The Misses, as children. Owned by Mrs. E. Wigglesworth.

Cheney — *Continued:* 15

114. Wolcott, Roger. Drawn 1854. Owned by Mrs. J. H. Wolcott.
115. Woodbridge. Owned by Mrs. E. Sherman.

CHURCH, FREDERICK EDWIN

b. *May 4, 1826, Hartford, Connecticut;* d. *April 7, 1900, New York.*
Landscape painter.

He was a pupil of Thomas Cole at Catskill. He was elected N. A. in 1849. From 1853 to 1857 he was in South America. "The Heart of the Andes," "Chimborazo" and "Niagara Falls" are the titles of some of his best known landscapes.

1. Cole, Thomas. (1801-1848.) Pencil. Reproduced in New York Times: Book Review and Magazine, October 9, 1921.

COLE, THOMAS

b. *February 1, 1801, Bolton-le-Moor, England;* d. *February 11, 1848, Catskill, New York.*
Landscape painter.

He was the only son of James and Mary Cole. Both Dunlap and Tuckerman give extended accounts of Thomas Cole. He made portraits in black lead pencil until 1820. After that year he devoted his time to landscape painting.

COLLIER, J. HOWARD

Flourished 1850-1857, Philadelphia and Boston.
Crayon portrait draughtsman.

He exhibited a crayon "Portrait of a Gentleman" at the Pennsylvania Academy in 1850.

Church — Collier: 16

15

COLYER, Vincent

b. *1825, Bloomingdale, now New York City;* d. *July 12, 1888, Contentment Island, Connecticut.*
Crayon portrait draughtsman and landscape painter.

He was made associate N. A. in 1849. He studied under J. R. Smith. Before the Civil War he lived in New York City.

COOPER, Peregrine F.

Flourished 1840-1890, Philadelphia.
Portrait painter in oils and miniature and portrait draughtsman in pastels.

Peregrine F. Cooper published a book in 1863 called "The Art of Making and Coloring Ivory Types, Photographs, Talbotypes, and Miniature Painting on Ivory. . . . by P. F. Cooper, Miniature, Portrait, Pastil, and Equestrian Painter and Photographer." He states in his introduction that he has had "the experience of twenty-three years in study and practice in miniature painting, twelve years of that time principally devoted to Talbotype, or Photograph and Ivorytype coloring." He exhibited at the Pennsylvania Academy.

COPLEY, John Singleton

b. *July 3, 1737, Boston;* d. *September 9, 1815, London, England.*
Historical painter, portrait painter in oils and miniature and portrait draughtsman in pastel.

John Singleton Copley was the son of Irish parents who arrived in Boston in 1736. The father died in the West Indies shortly after his son was born. In 1748 Mrs. Copley married again and the stepfather, Peter Pelham, who was both a painter and engraver gave the boy his first lessons in drawing. When he was fifteen he had already painted his first portraits. His success came early and Trumbull wrote in his "Autobiography" of the comfort of Copley's circumstances. In 1766 Copley sent the portrait of his half brother, Henry Pelham, to the exhibition in London where it was exhibited on account of its excellence in spite of the fact that it was sent anonymously and therefore subject to refusal. Through West's influence, he was elected a Fellow of the Society of Artists and invited to London. In 1769 he married Miss Susannah Clarke whose father was the owner of the famous shipment of tea destroyed in 1773 by the "Boston Tea Party." At one time Copley tried to quiet the mob who rough handled his father-in-law. The recollection of excesses committed by the "Sons of Liberty" made him later urge his half brother to resist conscription by force if necessary. From June to December, 1771, he was painting a number of portraits in New York. In 1774 he left for Europe on the eve of the Battle of Bunker's Hill. He was never to return. He went first to England and then to Italy. In Rome he started the large family portrait of Ralph Izard and his wife. From Genoa he wrote: "Genoa is a lovely city! If I should be suddenly transported to Boston I should think it only a collection of wren boxes." He probably passed through Swit-

Copley — *Continued:* 18

zerland in 1775. There is a portrait by Copley of the great Swiss pastellist Liotard and there are a few references to that artist in the "Copley Pelham" correspondence published by the Massachusetts Historical Society. Copley then visited Germany, Holland, and France and finally settled in London. He was elected R. A. in 1779. An extensive check list of his work was published by H. W. Bayley.

Copley's earlier pastels have a general bluish tone.

1. Amory, Thomas. (1682-1728.) Pastel. Bust portrait. Owned by Miss M. P. Codman, Bristol, Rhode Island. Copy of an earlier portrait by another artist.

2. Andrews, John. Crayon. Formerly owned by Reverend G. B. Andrews, Highwood.

3. Apthorp, Captain R. N. Crayon. Small size. Formerly owned by Miss A. Apthorp, Jamaica Plains.

4. Barrell, Joseph. (b. 1740.) Pastel. 22 x 17. Owned by Worcester Art Museum.

5. Barrell, Mrs. Joseph, née Anna Pierce. Pastel. 23 x 17. Owned by Mrs. W. A. Putnam, Brooklyn, New York. Reproduced in: Burlington Magazine, May, 1907.

6. Barrell, Mrs. Joseph, née Anna Pierce. Pastel. 23 x 17. Owned by Miss D. Keep.

7. Barrell, Mrs. Joseph, née Hannah Fitch, the second wife of Joseph Barrell. Pastel. 24 x 19. Owned by Mrs. C. H. Joy, Boston.

8. Brown, Mrs. Gawen, née Elizabeth Byles. (1737-1763.) Pastel. 17½ x 14½. Signed: "J. S. C., 1763." Formerly owned by C. H. Hart. Reproduced in Catalogue: Thomas B. Clarke collection, 1919. Now owned by R. C. and N. M. Vose, Boston.

9. Cabot, George. (1751-1823.) Drawn 1767. Small pastel. Owned in Brookline, Massachusetts, 1915.

10. Chardon, Peter. Pastel. Formerly owned by Mr. E. Brooks, Boston.

Copley — *Continued:* 19

FITZ GREENE HALLECK
BY HENRY INMAN
The New York Historical Society

11. Cooper, Reverend Samuel. (1725-1783.) Crayon. Formerly owned by Mr. Hixon, New York.
12. Cooper, Miss. Pastel. Owned by Mrs. Taylor, Worcester.
13. Copley, John Singleton. (1737-1815.) Pastel. 23 x 17. Owned by Mr. H. Amory, Boston.
14. Copley, Mrs. John Singleton, née Susan Clarke. Pastel. Oval. Owned by Mrs. F. G. Dexter, Boston.
15. Dumaresque, Mrs. Philip, née Rebecca Gardiner. (1745-1813.) Drawn 1763. Crayon. Oval. Owned by Mrs. W. A. Wadsworth, Boston.
16. Eliot, Josiah. Crayon. Formerly owned by Miss Hull, Fairfield, Connecticut.
17. Everett, Dr. Moses. Pastel. Owned by Miss A. Davis, Boston.
18. Gore Catherine, later Mrs. Samuel Torrey. Crayon. Owned by Miss F. Morse, Boston.
19. Green, Mrs. Edward, née Mary Storer, later Mrs. Benjamin Hall. (1736-d. after 1791.) Pastel. 23 x 17½. Signed: "John S. Copley, February, 1765." Owned by Metropolitan Museum. Reproduced in Metropolitan Museum Bulletin, 1908, p. 37.
20. Green, Joseph. (1703-1765.) Pastel. Owned by Boston Museum of Fine Arts.
21. Green, Councillor Joseph. (1706-1780.) Pastel. Loaned by Miss H. E. Snow to Boston Museum. Reproduced in Windsor: Memorial History of Boston, v. 3, p. 132.
22. Greene, Joseph. (b. 1745.) Pastel. 22 x 18. Drawn 1767.
23. Greene, Mrs. Joseph, née Miss Greene. Pastel. 22 x 18. Drawn 1767. Both Greene portraits owned by Mr. J. M. Forbes, Boston.
24. Hall, Hugh. 18 x 16. Drawn 1758. Crayon. Formerly owned by Miss Baurey, Boston.
25. Hancock, Thomas. (1703-1764.) Crayon. Owned by Mrs. J. W. Tilton.
26. Hancock, Thomas. (1703-1764.) 18 x 15. Crayon. Owned by Mrs. C. H. Wood.

Copley — *Continued:* 20

27. Hancock, Mrs. Thomas, née Lydia Henchman. (d. 1777.) 18 x 15. Owned by Mrs. J. W. Tilton, Haverhill, Massachusetts.

28. Henshaw, Sarah, later Mrs. Joseph Henshaw. Pastel. Formerly owned by Mr. S. W. Haywood.

29. Hill, Henry. (1736-1828.) Pastel. 23 x 17. Formerly owned by Mrs. Todd, Cambridge, Massachusetts.

30. Hill, Mrs. Henry, née Anna Barrett. (1740-1822.) 23 x 17. Owned by estate of Mrs. S. Barrett, 1915.

31. Holyoke, Edward. (1689-1769.) 18 x 16. Crayon. Owned by Mrs. R. King, Montclair, New Jersey.

32. Hutchinson, Thomas. (1711-1780.) A pencil portrait by Copley of Thomas Hutchinson is referred to in Copley's letter to Henry Pelham, August, 1774.

33. Jackson, Jonathan. (1743-1810.) Crayon. Bust. Owned by Mrs. Oliver W. Holmes, 1881.

34. Jackson, Jonathan. (1743-1810.) Pastel. 23 x 17. Drawn between 1761-1773. Owned by Colonel H. Lee, 1881. Reproduced in Windsor: Memorial History of Boston, v. 4, p. 154.

35. Jenkins, Mrs. Louis, née Miss Hooper. Pastel. 23 x 18. Owned by Miss S. Currier, Newburyport, Massachusetts.

36. Liotard, Jean Etienne. (1702-1790.) Pastel. Owned by Mr. A. Jarvis, Toronto, Canada, 1915.

37. Mayhew, Reverend Jonathan. (1720-1766.) Crayon. Destroyed by fire in 1872.

38. Murray, Reverend John. (1742-1793.) Pastel. Owned by Newbury Historical Society.

39. Pelham, Henry. (1749-1806.) Black crayon drawing 7⅜ x 6½. Signed: "JSC, 1767." Owned by Mr. H. P. Curtis, Boston, 1915. Now owned by Mr. Lawrence Park.

40. Pepperell, Sir William. (1746-1816.) 16¾ x 11. Pastel. Owned by Mr. E. P. Wheeler, New York.

41. Phillips, Mary Winthrop. Pastel. Owned by Mr. F. C. Weld, Lowell, Massachusetts.

Copley — *Continued*: 21

42. Powell, John. (1716-1794.) Crayon. 25 x 20.
43. Powell, Mrs. John, née Janet Grant. Crayon. 25 x 20. Both Powell portraits owned by Mr. A. Jarvis, Toronto, Canada.
44. Royall, Polly. A bill written by Henry Pelham to Isaac Royall notes "To a portrait in crayons of Miss Polly Small, Royall 5£ 12s."
45. Small, Captain John. (1726-1796.) Crayons. Drawn for Philip Dumaresque about 1768.
46. Small, Captain John. (1726-1796.) Crayons. Copy of the foregoing by Copley. Drawn for Captain John Small.
47. Smith, Reverend William. 23½ x 18½. Pastel. Loaned by Mr. R. C. Greenleaf to Metropolitan Museum, 1913-1921.
48. Storer, Ebenezer. (1699-1761.) 23 x 17. Pastel. Owned by Mr. W. S. Carter, New York.
49 Storer, Mrs. Ebenezer, née Mary Edwards. (1700-1771.) Crayon. 1769. Owned by Miss G. G. Eaton, Boston.
50. Temple, Sir John. Crayon. Signed: "J. S. Copley, 1764." Formerly owned by Mr. W. Tappan, Boston.
51. Temple, Lady, née Elizabeth Bowdoin. Crayon. Formerly owned by Mr. W. Tappan, Boston.
52. Traille, Robert. Drawn about 1762. 20 x 16. Owned by Dr. A. C. Heffinger, Portsmouth, New Hampshire.
53. Turner, Captain William. (1745-d. after 1787.) 23 x 17. Crayon. Formerly owned by Mr. S. F. Turner, Baltimore, Maryland.
54. Tyler, John Tyng. (d. 1767.) Pastel. 22 x 17. Owned by Mr. F. S. Whitwell, Boston. Portrait of a child.
55. Ward, Richard. (1689-1763.) Pastel. Owned by Rhode Island School of Design. Signed and dated 1754. Reproduced in Rhode Island School of Design: Bulletin, January 1918.
56. Wentworth, Sir John. (1737-1820.) Pastel. 22 x 18. Signed and dated 1769. Formerly owned by Mrs. G. Abbott.

Copley — *Continued: 22*

57. Whitworth, Dr. Crayon. Owned by Mr. J. D. W. White, Germantown, Pennsylvania.
58. Portrait of a Lady. Crayon. Exhibited in 1768 in London.

CRANCH, JOHN

b. *February 2, 1807, Washington, D. C.; d. January 1, 1891, Urbano, Ohio.*
Portrait painter.

He was the brother of C. P. Cranch, the author and artist. See Dunlap's "History."

1. Greenleaf, Nancy, later Mrs. C. P. Cranch. Reproduced in L. C. Scott: Life and Letters of C. P. Cranch.

DARLEY, FELIX OCTAVIUS CARR

b. *June 23, 1822, Philadelphia; d. March 27, 1888, Claymont, Delaware.*
Illustrator.

F. O. C. DARLEY, the son of John Darley the actor, started work at the age of fourteen in a counting house but soon attracted attention by his drawings and became well known as an illustrator. He illustrated the works of Irving, Dickens, Cooper, Simms, Longfellow and Shakespeare. He visited Europe about the end of the Civil War and returned in 1868. See Tuckerman: "Book of the Artists."

1. Bull, Ole. On his first visit to America. Drawing. Reproduced in M. C. Crawford: Romantic Days in Old Boston.
2. Cranch, Mrs. Christopher Pearse. Pencil. Reproduced in L. C. Scott: Life and letters of C. P. Cranch.

Cranch — Darley: 23

DOYLE, William M. S.

b. *1769, Boston;* d. *there May, 1828.*
Silhouettist, portrait painter in oils and miniature and crayon portrait draughtsman.

Doyle was the son of a British army officer stationed in Boston. He associated as a young man with Daniel Bowen the silhouettist at the "Bunch of Grapes Tavern." In 1805 the Boston directory states that he was a "miniature painter at the Columbia Museum." He was president of this institution. See Ethel S. Bolton: "Wax Portraits and Silhouettes."

1. Stillman, Samuel. "Drawn by Doyle-Annin & Smith Sc."

DUBOURJAL, Savinien Edme

b. *February 12, 1795, Paris;* d. *there 1853.*
Portrait painter in oils and miniature and portrait draughtsman in pencil.

A pupil of Girodet and a student at the École des Beaux Arts, Dubourjal first exhibited at the Salon in 1814. In 1846 he was in Boston and from 1847 to 1850 he was in New York exhibiting frequently at the National Academy Exhibitions. He is best known by his pencil and water color portraits. Some account of his friendship with G. P. A. Healy is given in the "Life of Healy" by Healy's daughter.

1. Webster, Caroline Leroy. Drawn 1845. Pencil. Owned by Mrs. A. Lawrence, Boston. Reproduced in McClure's Magazine, May 1897, p. 630.

Doyle — Dubourjal: 24

DUGGAN, Peter Paul

b. *before 1870, Ireland;* d. *October 15, 1861, Paris.*
Portrait painter in oils and crayon portrait draughts-
man.

About 1810 Duggan came to the United States
as a professional artist. He taught at the New York
Academy but was compelled on account of ill health
to abandon both teaching and painting. In 1845 he
sent a portrait to the Royal Hibernian Academy
Exhibition in Dublin. He later left America, went
to England and finally to Paris.

In a footnote in Windsor's "Memorial History of
Boston," v. 4, p. 393 concerning portraits of Wash-
ington Allston is the following: ". . . . a head by
Paul Duggan for the American Art Union Medal."

DUNLAP, William

b. *February 17, 1766, Perth Amboy, New Jersey;* d.
September 28, 1839, New York.
Dramatist, art historian, portrait painter in oils and
miniature and pastel portrait draughtsman.

As early as 1783, Dunlap made a crayon portrait
from life of George Washington. From 1784 to 1787
he was in England spending a brief time with West
and most of his time in aimless travels. However,
he painted portraits successfully in New York after
his return. From 1789 to 1805 he abandoned art,
entered civic affairs, then was a merchant, and finally became both a dramatist and theater manager.
His play "André" was first performed in 1798.

Bankruptcy, wanderings about the country exhibiting his religious compositions and chance portrait painting occupied his life until 1830 when he settled permanently in New York. In 1831 he was elected vice president of the National Academy which position he retained until 1838. The loss of one eye was a serious handicap to his work. He will be remembered for his "History of the Arts of Design in the United States," the best known source book for information concerning the early American artists. Oral S. Coad's "William Dunlap" contains a check list of his paintings.

1. Van Horne, John. Drawn 1783. Crayon.
2. Van Horne, Mrs. John. Drawn 1783. Crayon.
3. Washington, George. Drawn 1783. Crayon.

DURAND, ASHER BROWN

b. *August 21, 1796, Jefferson Village, now Maplewood, New Jersey;* d. *there September 17, 1886.*
Engraver, portrait painter and landscape painter.

The most eminent American engraver, one of the "Hudson River School" of landscape painters, and portrait painter. He was the son of a watch maker of Huguenot descent. He engraved for Peter Maverick for five years, then became his partner. Two of his most celebrated engravings were "The Declaration of Independence" after Trumbull and "Ariadne" after Vanderlyn. In 1835 he abandoned engraving and devoted his time entirely to painting. He was a charter member and very active in the affairs of the National Academy and was president

Durand: 26

from 1845 to 1861. His biography was written by John Durand.

1. Paulding, William. (1769-1854.) Drawn and engraved by Durand in 1826. Stauffer No. 631.
2. Pekenino, Michael. (flourished 1820-22.) Engraver. "Drawn and engraved by his friend A. B. Durand, New York, 1820." Stauffer No. 632.

DU SIMITIÈRE, PIERRE EUGENE

b. *1736*(?), *Geneva, Switzerland;* d. *October, 1784, Philadelphia.*

Naturalist, portrait painter in oils and miniature, and portrait draughtsman in pencil.

From about 1756 to 1765, Du Simitière lived in the West Indies. He then went to New York and in 1766 to Philadelphia. He resisted conscription in 1777 and was compelled to pay a heavy fine. In 1780 he opened his museum of curiosities. In 1781 he received an honorary M. A. degree from Princeton University. Thirteen small portrait drawings that he made of Benedict Arnold (1741-1801); Silas Deane (1737-1789); John Dickinson (1732-1808); William Henry Drayton (1742-1779); Horatio Gates (1728-1806); Samuel Huntington (1732-1796); John Jay (1745-1829); Henry Laurens (1724-1792); Baron von Steuben (1730-1794); Robert Morris (1734-1806); Joseph Reed (1741-1785); and George Washington (1732-1799) were engraved by Reading and published in London. These are reproduced in Windsor's "Memorial History of Boston." Some were engraved by B. L. Prevost of Paris. Most of them are in profile.

Du Simitière: 27

CAPT. JOHN DEARBORN
BY PIERRE EUGENE DU SIMITIERE
Collection of Mr. Charles A. Munn

1. Dearborn, Captain John. Pastel. Owned by Mrs. Charles A. Munn, N. Y., 1922.
2. Page, Sarah Dearborn. Pastel. Owned by Mr. Charles A. Munn, N. Y., 1922.

DUVIVIER AND SON

Flourished 1796-1797, Philadelphia.
Pastel portrait draughtsmen and painters on silk.

In Claypoole's "American Daily Advertiser," Philadelphia, October 31, 1797, page 3, column 3, their advertisement runs as follows: "ACADEMY OF DRAWING AND PAINTING. DUVIVIER & SON. Respectfully inform the public in general, but particularly their former pupils, that their academy will be again opened tomorrow, November 1st, for the reception of their pupils as well as others, who may place themselves under their tuition, to acquire the pleasing and useful art of Drawing and Painting, at No. 12 Strawberry Street, between Second and Third Streets near Market," and so on.

1. Hazard, Ebenezer. Pastel. Drawn 1796.
2. Hazard, Mrs. Ebenezer. Pastel. Drawn 1796. Both owned by Reverend F. E. Vermilye, New York, 1892. Both reproduced in C. W. Bowen: Centennial of Inauguration of Washington, pp. 156 and 51.

FAIRMAN, GIDEON

b. *June 26, 1774, Newton, Connecticut;* d. *March 18, 1827, Philadelphia.*
Engraver.

When he was a boy, Fairman worked as a jeweler and engraver in Albany. In 1810 he settled permanently in Philadelphia except for a stay in England that lasted from 1819 to 1822. During the War of 1812 he entered the army as a captain and finally became colonel. His brothers, David (1782-1815) and Richard (1787-1821) were also engravers. Gideon Fairman was a partner of Cephas G. Childs during 1824 in the firm of Fairman and Childs.

    1. Hamilton, Alexander. (1754-1804.) Pencil drawing. Reproduced in C. W. Bowen: Centennial of Inauguration of Washington, p. 25. Owned by Mr. R. M. Hamilton, New York, 1892.

FERRIS, Stephen, Jr.
Flourished 1857-1860, Philadelphia.
Crayon portrait draughtsman.

FIELD, Robert
b. *before 1794, Gloucester, England;* d. *August 9, 1819, Jamaica, West Indies.*
Engraver and portrait painter in oils and miniature.

    Nothing is known of Field's life before his arrival at London in 1794, except that he came from Gloucester. April of the same year he sailed for Baltimore, leaving shortly for New York. In 1795 he was in Philadelphia and visited Mount Vernon. In 1798 Rembrandt Peale records seeing him at Centreville, Maryland. In 1805 he was in Boston, sailing in 1808 for Halifax, Nova Scotia. In 1818 he sailed to London, leaving the next year for Jamaica where he died. Mr. Harry Piers in the "Nova Scotia Historical Society Collections," volume

18, has written an extensive account of Field. A number of his miniatures are listed in "Early American Portrait Painters in Miniature." He ranks as one of the finest American miniature painters.

1. Gallego, Mr. In Sulley's "Register" of his portraits a painting of "Mr. Gallego from a drawing by Field" is noted.

FISHER, J. J.
Flourished 1850, Petersburg, Virginia.
Crayon portrait draughtsman.

FLORIMONT, Austin
Flourished 1781, Philadelphia.
Miniature painter and crayon portrait draughtsman.

FRASER, Charles
b. *August 20, 1782, Charleston, South Carolina;* d. *there October 15, 1860.*
Portrait painter in miniature and oils.

CHARLES FRASER ranks with the greatest American miniature painters: Malbone, Trott and Field. He entered Charleston College about 1792, graduated in 1798, studied in a law office until 1800 and then devoted himself for a time to art, probably encouraged by the example of his friend Malbone. However after three years, he resumed his law studies. In 1807 he was admitted to the bar. After eleven years of practice he accumulated a competence, deserted the law permanently and again became an artist. He lived in Charleston almost all his life except for a few visits to Boston, New York and Co-

Fisher—Fraser: 30

lumbia, South Carolina. In 1857 his friends and admirers formed an exhibition of more than three hundred examples of his work. See the excellent illustrated article by Miss Alice R. H. Smith in "Art in America," June, 1915. In "Early American Portrait Painters in Miniature" more pages are devoted to Fraser than to any other artist.

1. Ramsay, David. (1749-1815.) "Engraved by J. B. Longacre from the drawing by C. Frazer (sic.) after a painting by C. W. Peale," for Longacre: National Portrait Gallery.

FULTON, ROBERT

b. *November 14, 1765, Little Britain, now Fulton, Pennsylvania;* d. *February 23, 1815, New York.*
Inventor and portrait painter in oils and miniature.

The Fultons came from Kilkenny, Ireland, before 1735. In 1785 Robert Fulton is listed in the Philadelphia directories as a miniature painter. In 1786 he sailed for London and received assistance from West. From 1791 to 1793 he exhibited at the Royal Academy and the Society of Artists. The latter year he was in Devonshire still painting. But by now he was fairly engrossed in mechanical experiments. His later life is that of an inventor although he occasionally resumed his brush. See A. C. Sutcliffe: "Robert Fulton."

1. Baldwin, Abraham. (1754-1807.) "Engraved by J. B. Forrest from a drawing by E. G. Leutze after an original sketch by R. Fulton."
2. Fulton, Robert. (1765-1815.) 8½ x 7½. Pencil draw-

Fulton: 31

ing. Inscribed: "To Henry Eckford with my friendship — this portrait of myself — Robert Fulton."

3. Ross, Margaret. Pastel. Drawn 1787. Owned by Mrs. C. S. Bradford, Philadelphia.

FURNASS, William Henry

b. *May 21, 1828, Philadelphia;* d. *March 4, 1867, Cambridge, Massachusetts.*

Portrait painter and crayon portrait draughtsman.

He studied two years in Europe at Düsseldorf, Munich, Dresden, Venice and Paris. After a brief stay in Philadelphia he settled in Boston. See Tuckerman: "Book of the Artists." Speaking of his crayon portraits Tuckerman notes: "In the estimation of many he stood next to Cheney in this line." Tuckerman mentions many of his portraits but it is difficult to tell whether they are crayons or oils.

1. May, Edith. Crayon. Engraved by J. Cheney.

GOVE, Elma Mary

Flourished 1851-1855, New York.

Portrait draughtsman in crayons.

HAINES, William

b. *June 21, 1778, Bedhampton, England;* d. *July 24, 1848, East Brixton, England.*

Engraver, portrait painter in miniature and oils, and portrait draughtsman in pencil.

Haines was apprenticed to Thew, the engraver, before leaving England in 1800 for the Cape of Good Hope. He later came to Philadelphia where

Furnass — Haines: 32

he stayed until 1805 when he returned to England.
See "Dictionary of National Biography."

1. Rush, Benjamin. (1745-1813.) "Drawn by W. Hains.
   Engraved by W. R. Jones." Owned by Mr. W. J. Campbell, 1913.
2. Wister, Casper. (1761-1818.) "Drawn and engraved by
   W. Haines." Owned by Mr. W. J. Campbell, Pa., 1913.
3. Barton, Dr. Benjamin Smith. Drawing sold at Henkel's,
   Pa., in 1913. Buyer Mr. Robert Fridenberg.

HALL, HENRY BRYAN

b. *March 11, 1808, London;* d. *April 25, 1884, Mor-
risonia, New York.*
Engraver and portrait painter in oils and miniature.

He was a pupil of Hoppner Meyer. He made the
drawings in pencil and wash for Dr. Thomas Addis
Emmett's series of privately printed "Club" portraits of the signers of the Declaration of Independence and other Revolutionary characters which he
also engraved.

HANLEY, W. H.

Flourished 1850-1856, Boston.
Portrait draughtsman in crayon.

HARTWELL, ALONZO

b. *February 19, 1805, Littleton, Massachusetts;* d.
January 17, 1873, Waltham, Massachusetts.
*Portrait painter in oils and crayon portrait draughts-
man.*

HARTWELL moved to Boston in 1822, was apprenticed to a wood engraver and practiced that art pro-

Hall — Hartwell: 33

fessionally from 1826 to 1851. The latter year he started painting portraits in oils.

1. Hoar, Elizabeth. Crayon. Reproduced in Emerson: Journal, v. 6.

HATHAWAY, Dr. R.

Flourished 1793.

A lithograph of Colonel Briggs Alden (1723-1796), lithographed by Tappan and Bradford is inscribed, Dr. R. Hathaway, del., 1793.

HAZLITT, John

b. *1767, baptised July 6, Marshfield, England;* d. *May 16, 1837, Stockport, England.*
Portrait painter in oils and miniature and portrait draughtsman in pastel.

The brother of William Hazlitt the essayist. John Hazlitt came to America in 1783 with his father, mother, brother and sister. The family moved extensively but for the most part they lived near or in Boston. In 1785 John Hazlitt advertised an art school with Joseph Dunkerley in Boston. He went frequently to Hingham, Weymouth, and Salem. The father returned to England in 1786 and the family joined him in 1787. See Essex Institute Historical Collections, October, 1920.

1. Gay, Reverend Ebenezer. (1696-1787.) Drawn about 1785.

HERRING, James

b. *January 12, 1794, London, England;* d. *October, 1867, Paris, France.*
Engraver and portrait painter.

JAMES HERRING came to New York in 1804. His father kept a brewery on the Bowery. The boy colored maps both in New York and Philadelphia before finally painting portraits. His studio was on Chatham Square. He associated with Longacre in the "National Portrait Gallery" published in 1834-1839, an invaluable collection of engravings from portraits of eminent Americans. His son Frederick William Herring was also a portrait painter.

1. Madison, Mrs. James, née Dorothea Payne. "Drawn by J. Herring after J. Wood. Engraved by J. F. E. Prud-'homme."
2. Morgan, Daniel. "Drawn by J. Herring from Colonel Trumbull's sketch. Engraved by J. F. E. Prud'homme."
3. Rutledge, John. (1739-1800.) "Engraved by G. F. Storm from a drawing by James Herring after the original by Colonel Trumbull."
4. Wayne, Anthony. (1745-1796.) "Drawn by James Herring from a sketch by Colonel J. Trumbull. Engraved by J. F. E. Prud'homme."

HOFFY, ALFRED

Flourished 1840-1852, Philadelphia.
Portrait painter, crayon portrait draughtsman and lithographer.

HOFFY exhibited at the Pennsylvania Academy for a number of years.

HUNTINGTON, DANIEL

b. *October 14, 1816, New York City;* d. *there April 18, 1906.*
Portrait, historical and landscape painter.

PORTRAIT OF HIMSELF
BY ROBERT FULTON

Educated at Hamilton College and New York University. In 1835 he studied under Morse and later under F. R. Spencer. He visited Paris, Florence and Rome from 1839 to 1840. He lived in Florence from 1843 to 1845, and in 1851 he visited London. He was president of the National Academy from 1862 to 1869 and from 1877 to 1891. Mr. George D. Smith purchased over a thousand pencil studies for portraits by Huntington at a sale at Anderson's Art Galleries in New York.

INMAN, HENRY

b. *October 28, 1801, Utica, New York;* d. *January 17, 1846, New York.*
Portrait painter in oils and miniature.

As a boy Inman received drawing lessons from an itinerant artist in Utica. When the family moved to New York about 1812 the boy continued his drawing studies at a day school. A military career was planned for him but a chance visit with his father to the studio of John Wesley Jarvis resulted in his becoming that painter's apprentice. The Master and pupil made frequent visits to various cities, young Inman painting the backgrounds to his master's portraits and together they often finished a portrait a day. In 1822 after a stay in Boston his apprenticeship was over. He took a studio on Vesey Street, married and soon established himself as a professional portrait painter. He was vice president of the National Academy from 1826-1830 and from 1838 to 1844. From 1831 to 1835 he lived at

Inman: 36

35

Mt. Holly, New Jersey and Philadelphia. In 1843 his health broke and he sailed for England with commissions to paint Macauley, Chalmers and Wordsworth. The voyage and the change revived his health but upon his return late in 1845 he again fell ill and died the following year. Tuckerman gives a long account of Inman in his "Book of Artists."

1. Halleck, Fitz-Greene. (1790-1867.) 5x3½. Pencil. Owned by the New York Historical Society.

2. Halleck, Fitz-Greene. (1790-1867.) Evidently a drawing. Engraved by Parker for Wilson: Brayant and his Friends, p. 245.

3. Morris, George Perkins. (1802-1864.) Evidently a drawing. Engraved by Burt for Wilson: Bryant and his Friends, p. 403.

4. Hoffman, Charles Fenno. Pen sketch. At the Inman Exhibition in 1846 and then owned by H. T. Tuckerman. Engraved by A. L. Dick.

5. Porter, William T. Crayon. At the Inman Exhibition in 1846 and then owned by W. T. Porter. Engraved by H. W. Smith. Frontispiece to Life of W. T. Porter, N. Y., 1860.

6. Inman, Henry. "Colossal crayon. Portrait from the bust by Ball Hughes." At the Inman Exhibition of 1846 and then owned by Mr. McMuntrie.

JACKSON, John Adams

b. *1825, Bath, Maine;* d. *1879.*
Sculptor and crayon portrait draughtsman.

He was a pupil of D. C. Johnson. In 1851 he started making portrait busts.

Jackson: 37

JANVIER, A. W.

Flourished 1858, Philadelphia.
Crayon portrait draughtsman.

JARVIS, John Wesley

b. *1780, South Shields, England;* d. *January 14, 1839, New York.*
Portrait painter in oils and miniature and pencil portrait draughtsman.

As a boy Jarvis was left in the care of his maternal uncle, John Wesley, the founder of Methodism. In 1795 he was taken to Philadelphia by his father. He was apprenticed to Savage the engraver and moved with his master to New York in 1800. In 1802 he set up independently as an engraver. From 1804 to 1809 he formed a miniature painting partnership with Joseph Wood at number 40 Nassau Street. In 1810 Jarvis visited Charleston, in 1811 he visited Baltimore. He exhibited portraits in Philadelphia in 1813 and 1814. The latter year Henry Inman became his apprentice and together they visited various cities from Boston to New Orleans. He sank into obscurity in his latter days and died in extreme poverty at the home of his sister, Mrs. Childs. In his earlier days however he was much sought after for his lively conversation and associated with such men as Irving and Randolph. Both Dunlap and Tuckerman give long accounts of Jarvis. He is mentioned in Irving's "Letters."

1. Irving, Washington. (1783-1859.)

Janvier — Jarvis: 38

JOHNSON, Eastman

b. *July 29, 1824, Lovell, Maine;* d. *April 5, 1906, New York.*

Genre and portrait painter and crayon portrait draughtsman.

He was the son of Philip C. Johnson, Secretary of State for Maine. He worked in a lithographic establishment in Boston in 1840 and after a year went to Augusta, Maine, where he commenced making portraits in black crayon. He also visited Newport. In 1845 the family moved to Washington, D. C., and young Johnson drew many crayon portraits working in the Senate Committee Rooms at the Capitol. He was in Boston from 1846 to 1849. From 1849 to 1851 he studied in Düsseldorf. The latter year he moved to the Hague where he stayed until 1855 when he moved to Paris. From 1856 to 1858 he lived again in Washington. In the autumn of 1858 he moved to New York where he remained the rest of his life except for a period spent in Boston and visits to Europe in 1885, 1891 and 1897. He was elected N. A. in 1860.

"The original is the best," Johnson used to say of his crayon portraits, "and that you cannot have." This accounts for the duplicate drawings. See "Scribner's," May, 1906; and "World's Work," December, 1906. He worked at one time in the Studio Building in Boston. Twenty-five dollars was the usual price he received for his crayon portraits.

Johnson: 39

1. Adams, John Quincy. (1767-1848.) Reproduced "World's Work," December, 1906. Owned by Mr. Albert Rosenthal.
2. Barnard, Frederick Augustus Porter. (1809-1889.) Owned by Mr. Albert Rosenthal.
3. Cannon, Le Grand, of New York. Owned by Mr. Albert Rosenthal.
4. De Peyster, Frederick. (1796-1862.) Owned by Mr. Albert Rosenthal.
5. Dobbin, James Cochran. (1814-1851.) Owned by Mr. Albert Rosenthal.
6. Emerson, Ralph Waldo. (1803-1882.)
7. Felton, Cornelius Conway. (1807-1862.)
8. Garet, Polly. Owned by Mr. Albert Rosenthal.
9. Goddard, Mrs. F. N. Owned by Mr. Albert Rosenthal.
10. Hamilton, Mrs. Alexander, née Elizabeth Schuyler. (1757-1854.) Drawn 1846. 14¾ x 12¾. Owned by New York Historical Society. Reproduced in McClure's Magazine, April, 1897, p. 513.
11. Hamilton, Mrs. Alexander. Drawn 1846. Owned by Mr. Albert Rosenthal.
12. Harrison, President Benjamin. (1833-1901.) Owned by Mr. Albert Rosenthal.
13. Hawthorne, Nathaniel. (1804-1864.)
14. Higginson, Thomas Wentworth. (b. 1823.) Reproduced in M. C. Crawford: Romantic Days in the Early Republic.
15. Hoffman, Dean Samuel P. Owned by Mr. Albert Rosenthal.
16. Holthrop, Mrs. Owned by Mr. Albert Rosenthal.
17. Jenkins, Nathaniel. 8½ x 6½. Mrs. E. Johnson sale, 1907.
18. Johnson, Eastman. Self portrait. Signed "E. J." Owned by Mr. Albert Rosenthal.
19. Kennedy, John Pendleton. (1795-1870.) Owned by Mr. Albert Rosenthal.

Johnson — *Continued:* 40

20. Kennedy, Robert Lenox. (b. 1822.) Owned by Mr. Albert Rosenthal.
21. Lincoln, Abraham. Crayon study for the celebrated painting: The Boy Lincoln. In: "Harry MacNeill Bland, Lincoln Collection."
22. Longfellow, Henry Wadsworth. (1807-1882.) Drawn 1846. Reproduced in C. Ticknor; Glimpses of Authors, p. 44.
23. Longfellow, Stephen. (1776-1849.)
24. Longfellow, Mrs. Stephen, née Zilpha Wadsworth.
25. Lottmer, Colonel. Owned by Mr. Albert Rosenthal.
26. McCosh, Mrs. James. Owned by Mr. Albert Rosenthal.
27. Manning, Daniel. (1831-1887.)
28. Madison, Mrs. James, née Dorothea Payne. 22½ x 16. Signed: "E. Johnson, March, 1846." Reproduced in "World's Work," December, 1906; sold at Mrs. E. Johnson sale, 1907.
29. Madison, Mrs. James. Replica of foregoing. Once owned by Daniel Webster.
30. Miles, General Nelson Appleton. (b. 1839.) Owned by Mr. Albert Rosenthal.
31. Munson, Judge. Owned by Mr. Albert Rosenthal.
32. Myrick, Captain. Owned by Mr. Albert Rosenthal.
33. Nash, Stephen Payne. Owned by Mr. Albert Rosenthal.
34. Pepoon, Mr. Owned by Kennedy and Company.
35. Persico, Lugi. Owned by Kennedy and Company.
36. Peters, Richard. (1780-1846.) Owned by Kennedy and Company.
37. Pierce, Mrs., née Miss Longfellow.
38. Sumner, Charles. (1811-1874.) 1846. Engraved by H. W. Reproduced in Webster: Writings and Speeches, v. 4, p. 464.
39. Webster, Daniel. (1782-1852.) Reproduced in "World's Work," December, 1906. Sold at Mrs. E. Johnson sale, 1907.
40. Webster, Daniel. (1782-1852.) Replica of foregoing. Owned by Governor Winthrop in 1886.

Johnson — *Continued:* 41

JOHNSON, Henrietta

d. *March 9, 1728-9, Charleston, South Carolina.*
Portrait draughtsman in pastels.

Reverend Robert Wilson in "Art and Artists in Provincial South Carolina" published in the Charleston "Year Book" for 1899, writes: "Whether Henrietta Johnson was maid or wife we do not know, but we owe her a debt of gratitude for leaving to us the counterfeit presentments of so many representatives of names famous in the early life of South Carolina."

1. Broughton, Lieut. Governor Thomas. (d. 1738.) Drawn 1712. Owned by Mr. Joseph F. Heyward, Oakley Station, S. C. Reproduced and described in C. K. Bolton: Portraits of the Founders. Also in G. C. Lee: History of North America, v. 3, p. 416.
2. Dwight, Mrs. Daniel, née Broughton.
3. De Lisle, Henrietta Charlotte.
4. De Lisle, Mademoiselle. Drawn 1711.
5. Gale, Chief Justice Christopher. (1680-1734.) Owned by Mr. William P. Little, Raleigh, N. C. Reproduced and described in C. K. Bolton: Portraits of the Founders.
6. Gibbes, Mrs. John, née Ann Broughton.
7. Mazyck, Mrs. Paul, née de Chastaigne.
8. Prioleau, Pastor Elias. Drawn 1715. Copy?
9. Prioleau, Mrs. Elias, née Jeanne Bourgeaud. Drawn 1715. Copy?
10. Ravenel, Mrs. Rene Louise, née Susanne Le Nolle. Drawn 1710.
11. Ravenel, Mrs. Daniel, née Damaris Elizabeth de St. Julien.
12. Taylor, Mrs. Robert, née Catherine Le Noble. Drawn 1710.
13. Wragg, Mrs. Drawn 1708.

Johnson: 42

14. Wragg, Mrs. Samuel. Drawn 1708.
15. Wragg, Mrs. William.

JOHNSTON, DAVID CLAYPOOLE

b. *March, 1797, Philadelphia;* d. *November 8, 1865, Dorchester, Massachusetts.*
Engraver and lithographer.

D. C. JOHNSTON was well known as a caricaturist and actor. He started as an engraver in Philadelphia about 1815. In 1825 he took to the stage for a while in Boston. Here he made a series of portrait drawings on stone of actors. The remaining years of his life he spent in Boston.

1. Allston, Washington. (1779-1843.) "From the engraving by David C. Johnston after his own drawing." Engraving reproduced in Dunlap: History, 1918 edition. Engraved for: The New Mirror.

JOHNSTON, JOHN

b. *about 1753, Boston;* d. *there June 28, 1818.*
Portrait and figure painter and portrait draughtsman in pastel.

Served in the Revolution under General Knox and was wounded at Brooklyn. He worked in Boston.

1. Flagg, Colonel Samuel. 19½ x 15¾. Owned by Mrs. Richard Ward Greene, Worcester, Massachusetts.
2. Johnston, John. Self portrait. Pastel. Reproduced in Dunlap: History, 1918 edition.

JOHNSTON, THOMAS MURPHY

Flourished 1856-1868, Boston.
Portrait draughtsman in crayons.

Johnston, D. — Johnston, T.: 43

GENERAL ANDREW JACKSON
BY THOMAS SULLY
Property of Mrs. Albert Sully, Brooklyn, N. Y.

The latter part of his life he lived in Dorchester. He was the son of David C. Johnston.

JUDKINS, Miss E. M.
Flourished about 1847.
Portrait draughtsman in crayons.
  1. Sales, Francis. (1777-1854.) Harvard.

KIMBERLEY, Denison
b. *1814, Guilford, Connecticut;* d. *after 1862.*
Engraver and portrait painter.

Studied engraving with G. H. Cushman under Asaph Willard and became a successful portrait line engraver. He abandoned engraving in 1858 and studied painting in Boston. In 1862 he lived in Hartford. See Stauffer: American Engravers.
  1. Cheney, Seth Wells. (1810-1856.) Charcoal Drawing. Owned by Mrs. E. D. Cheney, 1893.

KOSCIUSZKO, Tadeusz Andrzei Bonaventura
b. *February 12, 1746, Mereczowszcyzna, Lithuania;*
d. *October 15, 1817, Solothurn, Switzerland.*
Polish soldier who fought in the American Revolutionary Army.

General Gates said of Kosciuszko: "An able engineer and one of the best and neatest draughtsmen I ever saw." However from the beginning of his career as the hero of a romantic elopement to his tragic death caused by falling off a cliff while on horse back, Kosciuszko found little time to cultivate his talent. See A. W. W. Evans: "Memoir of Kosciuszko," privately printed, New York, 1883.

Judkins — Kosciuszko: 44

Against the praise of General Gates may be set the following from Dr. William Thornton who wrote to Jefferson in July, 1816, concerning the Kosciuszko crayon portrait: "Never was such injustice done to you except by sign painters and General Kosciuszko, than which last nothing could be so bad."

1. Alden, Judah. (1750-1845.) Drawn 1777. Outline in ink. Reproduced in Windsor: Memorial History of Boston, v. 3, p. 99.
2. Jefferson, Thomas. (1743-1826.) Crayon. The original lost. An aquatint in color by Sokolnicki owned by Mr. W. J. Campbell, Philadelphia, 1892. Reproduced in C. W. Bowen: Centennial of Inauguration of Washington.

LAMBDIN, George C.

b. *1830;* d. *1896.*
Portrait painter and crayon portrait draughtsman.

The son of J. R. Lambdin the portrait painter. He worked in Philadelphia.

LAMBDIN, James Reid

b. *May 10, 1807, Pittsburg, Pennsylvania;* d. *January 31, 1889, Philadelphia.*
Portrait painter in oils and miniature.

J. R. Lambdin studied under Sully during 1823-1825 and in the latter year established himself in his native city as a portrait painter, frequently visiting the south. In 1837 he settled in Philadelphia and taught at the University of Pennsylvania.

1. Tyler, John. (1790-1862.) "Engraved by J. B. Forrest from a drawing by J. R. Lambdin," for Longacre: National Portrait Gallery.

LAWRENCE, Samuel

b. *1812, Surrey, England;* d. *February 28, 1884, London, England.*
Portrait painter and crayon portrait draughtsman.

Samuel Lawrence was a very popular artist in London and drew many portraits; among them Browning, Thackeray, Carlyle, and Mrs. Gaskell. An obituary notice in the "Athenaeum" for March 8, 1884, where a number of his portraits are listed, states that the artist's name is variously spelled: Lawrence, Laurence, and Laurance. He visited the United States in 1854.

1. Bancroft, George. (1800-1891.) Owned by Worcester Art Museum. Reproduced in M. A. D. Howe: George Bancroft, v. 2.
2. Longfellow, Henry Wadsworth. (1807-1882.) Reproduced in Longfellow: Works, 1904, v. 2.

LAWRIE, Alexander, Jr.

b. *1828, New York City;* d. *after 1870.*
Portrait painter, engraver and crayon portrait draughtsman.

He exhibited a crayon portrait of Thomas Sully at the Pennsylvania Academy in 1854. He studied both at the National Academy and the Pennsylvania Academy. Later he studied with Leutze in Düsseldorf and Picot in Paris. Appleton's "Cyclopædia" notes that "He has made upward of a thousand crayon heads, including likenesses of Richard H. Stoddard and Thomas Buchanan Read." He was elected N. A. in 1866.

Lawrence — Lawrie: 46

LEMET, L.

Flourished 1804-1805, Philadelphia, New York and Albany.

Engraver and crayon portrait draughtsman.

Some of his portrait engravings were of Dr. Rush, Joseph Shippen and John Williams. Stauffer in his "American Engravers," quotes his advertisement from the "Albany Centinal" for November, 1805. The beginning of the notice reads: "L. Lemet respectfully informs the Ladies and Gentlemen of Albany that he takes Likenesses in Crayons, as large as life, and engraves them in a reduced size in a new and elegant manner." He advertised in the "New York Commercial Advertiser," March 15, 1805, where he calls himself the "late partner of Mr. St. Mesnin"—evidently meaning St. Memin. See W. Kelby: Notes on American Artists, p. 45.

LESLIE, ELIZA

b. *November, 1787, Philadelphia; d. January 2, 1858, Gloucester, New Jersey.*

Authoress and artist.

She was the sister of C. R. Leslie. She made a few crayon portraits.

LESLIE, CHARLES ROBERT

b. *October 17, 1794, London, England; d. there May 5, 1859.*

Historical and portrait painter.

Better known as an historical painter, C. R. Leslie's early work was a series of portrait drawings made as a boy in Philadelphia. He went to London in 1811 and lived there practically all his life. During 1831 he was instructor in drawing at West Point. He wrote the "Memoirs of John Constable." He drew a number of portraits engraved by David Edwin for "The Mirror of Taste."

1. Cooke, George Frederick. (1756-1811.) As Richard III. Drawing.
2. Cooke, George Frederick, as Othello. Drawing.

LONGACRE, James Barton

b. *August 11, 1794, Delaware County, Pennsylvania;*
d. *January 1, 1869, Philadelphia.*
Engraver, portrait painter in water colors, and portrait draughtsman in pencil.

Longacre was the descendant of a Swedish colonist who settled in Delaware. After serving an apprenticeship with Murray the engraver, he started professionally in 1819. From 1834 to 1839 he published, in association with James Herring, the "National Portrait Gallery," an invaluable source book of early American portraits. He was engraver for the United States mint from 1844 until his death. "Extracts from the Diary of James Barton Longacre" were published in the "Pennsylvania Magazine of History," for 1905. He there notes making several pencil portrait drawings later to be engraved. Engravings from the portrait drawings listed below are nearly all to be found in the "National Portrait Gallery." A number of portraits in sepia and pencil by James Barton Longacre are in the possession of Mrs. Augusta M. Longacre.

Longacre: 48

1. Adams, Samuel. (1722-1803.) "Drawn and Engraved by J. B. Longacre from a painting by Copley."
2. Adams, Samuel. (1722-1803.) "Engraved by G. F. Storm from a drawing by J. B. Longacre after Copley."
3. Barry, William T. (1785-1835.) "Drawn from Life and Engraved by James B. Longacre."
4. Bowditch, Nathaniel. (1773-1838.) "Engraved by J. Cross from a drawing by J. B. Longacre after the bust by Frazee."
5. Branch, James. "Drawn and engraved by J. B. Longacre."
6. Calhoun, John C. (1782-1850.) "Engraved by T. B. Welch from a Drawing by J. B. Longacre."
7. Carroll, Charles. (1737-1832.) "Drawn and engraved by J. B. Longacre from a painting by Field."
8. Cass, Lewis. (1782-1830.) "Engraved by E. Wellmore from a drawing by J. B. Longacre."
9. Chapman, Nicholas. "Drawn and engraved by J. B. Longacre."
10. Chase, Samuel. (1741-1811.) "Engraved by J. B. Forrest from a Drawing by J. B. Longacre after an original portrait by Jarvis."
11. Dale, Richard. (1756-1826.) "Engraved by R. W. Dodson from a drawing by J. B. Longacre after a portrait by J. Wood in Peale's Museum, New York.
12. Eaton, John H. "Drawn and engraved by J. B. Longacre."
13. Hayne, Robert Y. (1791-1841.) "Engraved by J. B. Forrest from an original Drawing from life by J. B. Longacre."
14. Hayne, Robert Y. (1791-1841.) "Engraved and Published by J. B. Longacre, Philadelphia, December, 1840. From an original drawing by himself taken from life A. D., 1830."
15. Jackson, Andrew. (1767-1845.) "Drawn from Life. September 23, 1829 and Engraved by J. B. Longacre."

Longacre—*Continued:* 49

Longacre painted a number of miniature portraits from this drawing for breast pins.

16. Jackson, Andrew. (1767-1845.) 1829. Drawing. Owned by Mrs. H. C. Wood, Philadelphia.

17. Jackson, James. "Engraved by W. A. Wilmer from a drawing by J. B. Longacre after St. Memin.

18. Jefferson, Thomas. (1743-1826.) "Drawn and Engraved by J. B. Longacre from the Portrait by Field after Stuart."

19. Livingston, Edward. (1764-1836.) "Engraved by E. Wellmore from a drawing by J. B. Longacre."

20. Madison, James. (1751-1836.) "Engraved by T. B. Welch from a drawing by J. B. Longacre taken from life at Mont Pelier, Va., July, 1833."

21. Marion, Francis. (1732-1795.) "Engraved by T. B. Welch from a drawing by J. B. Longacre after the portrait in a painting by T. Stothard, R. A., of the Battle of Eutaw."

22. Paine, Robert Treat. (1731-1814.) "Drawn and Engraved by J. B. Longacre from a Sketch by Savage."

23. Pickering, Timothy. (1745-1829.) "Engraved by T. B. Welch from a drawing by J. B. Longacre after G. Stuart."

24. Poinsett, Joel R. (1779-1851.) "Drawn from life and engraved by James B. Longacre."

25. Rutledge, Edward. (1749-1800.) "Drawn and Engraved by J. B. Longacre from a Painting by Earle."

26. Rutter, Martin. "Drawn from life and Engraved by J. B. Longacre."

27. St. Clair, Major General Arthur. (1734-1818.) "Engraved by E. Wellmore from a drawing by J. B. Longacre of the original by C. W. Peale."

28. Sargent, Dr. Thomas. "Drawn from Life and Engraved by J. B. Longacre."

29. Spencer, O. M. "Drawn from Life and Engraved by J. B. Longacre."

30. Van Buren, Martin. (1782-1862.) "Drawn from Life and

Longacre — *Continued:* 50

Engraved by J. B. Longacre. Published by B. O. Tyler, Washington City, 1830."

31. Watson, John Fanning. Pencil. Signed "J. B. Longacre, Del advivum, 1836." 5½ x 4¼. Owned by Mr. A. Rosenthal, 1920. Owned by Ehrich Galleries, 1922.

32. White, William. (1748-1836.) "Engraved by T. B. Welch from a Drawing by J. B. Longacre after G. Stuart."

33. Wirt, William. (1772-1834.) "Drawn from Life and Engraved by J. B. Longacre."

34. Woodbury, Levi. (1790-1851.) "Drawn from Life and Engraved by J. B. Longacre."

35. Wylie, Samuel B. "Drawn by J. B. Longacre from a Painting by J. Neagle, Philadelphia, 1836."

LOSSING, BENSON JOHN

b. *February 21, 1813, Beekman, N. Y.;* d. *June 3, 1891, Dover Plains, N. Y.*
Author.

He made hundreds of portrait drawings after paintings to illustrate his "Field Book of the Revolution," "Field Book of the War of 1812" and other volumes. See N. Paine: "Biographical Notice of Benson John Lossing, prepared for the Worcester Society of Antiquity," 1892.

LOUD, MRS. H. C.

Flourished 1850, Philadelphia.
Crayon portrait draughtsman.

MALBONE, EDWARD GREENE

b. *August, 1777, Newport, Rhode Island;* d. *May 7, 1807, Savannah, Georgia.*
Miniature painter.

Lossing — Malbone: 51

GOVERNOR RICHARD WARD
BY JOHN SINGLETON COPLEY
The R. I. School of Design, Providence, R. I.

MALBONE received instruction from Samuel King about 1792. The next year is the date of his first professional miniature. In 1794 he went to Providence, in 1796 he moved to Boston and in 1797 he visited New York. He was in Philadelphia for a short time in 1798 when the yellow fever epidemic compelled him to live outside the city. In 1800 he visited Charleston, South Carolina. From May to December, 1801, he studied in London, stopping at Charleston upon his return and sailing for Newport the spring of 1802. In 1803-1804 he was in New York. In 1804-1805 he was in Boston. In 1805-1806 he was in Charleston. March, 1806, he retired to Newport on account of ill health. December of that year he sailed for Jamaica but the climate proving without benefit he bought his passage for Newport and started home. However he left the ship at Savannah in a very weakened condition and died at the home of a cousin.

Malbone was the foremost American miniature painter. He also occasionally painted in oils and drew pastel portraits. One hundred and fifty-seven miniatures by him are listed in "Early American Portrait Painters in Miniature."

1. Whitehorne, Mrs. John. Pastel. Exhibition, Newport, Rhode Island, 1890.

MARTIN,
Flourished 1797, 1808, New York.
Portrait draughtsman in crayons.

MARTIN was an Englishman who came from Shef-

Martin: 52

field to New York about 1797. Although his work was poor it was in steady demand.

MARTIN, CHARLES

Flourished 1850-1851, Bristol, Rhode Island.
Portrait painter and crayon portrait draughtsman.

He exhibited at the National Academy in 1851.

1. Hamilton, Mrs. Alexander, née Elizabeth Schuyler. Drawn 1851. Life size. Owned by Mr. P. Schuyler, 1898. Reproduced in C. W. Bowen: Centennial of Inauguration of Washington, p. 57; also McClure's Magazine, April, 1897, p. 513; also A. H. Wharton: Colonial Days, p. 308.

MASON, GEORGE

Flourished 1768, Boston.
Limner and crayon portrait draughtsman.

He inserted an advertisement in the Boston "Chronicle" for June, 1768, stating that he drew portraits in crayon for two guineas each.

MASSON, EMILE

Flourished 1852-1856, Boston.
Crayon portrait draughtsman.

MILES, EDWARD

b. *October 14, 1752, Yarmouth, England;* d. *1828, Philadelphia.*
Miniature painter and crayon portrait draughtsman.

As a boy, Edward Miles was a messenger for a surgeon who encouraged him to study in London, where he went in 1771. He was employed by Sir Joshua Reynolds to make miniature copies of his portraits. During 1775-1779 he exhibited at the Royal Academy. He finally became painter to Queen Charlotte. In 1797 he went to Russia and was appointed court painter to Tsar Paul. In 1807 he settled in Philadelphia where he lived the rest of his life. The directory entries list him both as a drawing teacher and portrait painter in crayons.

NEGUS, CAROLINE

Flourished 1844-1856, Boston.
Crayon portrait draughtsman and portrait painter in miniature.

She married Richard Hildreth, the historian. She was a cousin of the artist, George Fuller and during the early forties shared a studio with him.

NEWSAM, ALBERT

b. *May 20, 1809, Steubenville, Ohio; d. November 20, 1864, near Wilmington, Del.*
Lithographer and portrait draughtsman.

He was a deaf mute, the son of a boat man. Left an orphan at an early age, a deaf imposter used his talent for drawing to make money. Then he was deserted by this man in Philadelphia, 1820. Here he was educated at the Institute for the Deaf and Dumb, where the authorities developed his talent under Bridport and Catlin. Under P. S. Duval he developed into a prolific portrait lithographer. See D. M. Stauffer: American Engravers. The Pennsylvania Magazine of History and Biography published an extended list of his lithographs compiled by Stauffer. See vols. 24-26, 1900-1902.

Negus — Newsam: 54

NEWTON, Gilbert Stuart

b. *September 21, 1795, Halifax, Nova Scotia;* d. *August 5, 1835, Chelsea, England.*

Genre and portrait painter.

He was the nephew of Gilbert Stuart and studied for a while under his uncle but proved a very unteachable pupil. He went to Italy, France and England and arrived in London in company with C. R. Leslie in 1817. Dunlap in his "History of the Arts of Design" gives an extended account of Newton and quotes Washington Irving's recollections of the artist.

> 1. Newton, Gilbert Stuart. (1795-1835.) Pencil outline. Profile self portrait. Signed: "G. S. Newton, 1821." Formerly owned by Charles Henry Hart. An etching from this profile by S. J. Ferris, reproduced in Dunlap: History, 1918 edition, v. 3, p. 78.

PEALE, Charles Willson

b. *April 16, 1741, Queen Ann's County, Maryland;* d. *February 22, 1827, Philadelphia.*

Portrait painter in oils and miniature.

Peale learned the trade of saddler in Annapolis. He was also a jeweler and cabinet maker by trade. In 1765 he went to Boston, where he met Copley; in 1766-7 he was in Virginia; and in the latter year he sailed for London to study under West. In 1774, he was again in Annapolis. In 1776, he was in Philadelphia. That year he became captain of a company of volunteers and saw service under Washington at Trenton and Germantown. He was a member of the Legislature in 1779. In 1802, he formed his famous "Peale's Museum." He painted a num-

Newton — Peale: 55

ber of portraits of Washington. He was a brother of James Peale and the father of Rembrandt Peale. Portions of his autobiography appeared in the "Pennsylvania Magazine of History," 1914.

1. Washington, George. (1732-1799.) Drawn from life, 1787. Owned by Historical Society of Pennsylvania.

PEASE, Joseph Ives

b. August 9, 1809, Norfolk, Connecticut; d. July 2, 1883, near Salisbury, Connecticut.
Engraver, water color painter and crayon portrait draughtsman.

He studied engraving under Oliver Pelton in Hartford. Two winters he studied crayon drawing at the National Academy in New York. He settled in Philadelphia in 1835 and lived there many years, popular both as a portrait draughtsman and teacher. See French: "Art and Artists of Connecticut." Also Stauffer: "American Engravers."

PERKINS, Miss

Flourished about 1790, Connecticut.
Portrait draughtsman in pastel.

She was a sister of Dr. Perkins. Portraits in pastel probably by her of Caleb Perkins, Lucy Perkins, and Sarah Perkins are owned by the Connecticut Historical Society.

PERSICO, Gennarino

Flourished 1822-1834, Philadelphia.
Miniature painter and drawing teacher.

He was the brother of Lugi Persico, the sculptor.

Pease — Persico: 56

He came from Naples. See "Lancaster Historical Society Papers," v. 16, No. 10.

    1. Louvilliere, Joseph Count de, after Vicard. Chalk drawing. Exhibited at the Pennsylvania Academy, 1827.

PINE, ROBERT EDGE

b. *between 1730 and 1742, London, England;* d. *November 19, 1788, Philadelphia.*
Portrait and historical painter.

Pine painted in England for sometime before coming with his family to America in 1784. Rembrandt Peale in his "Reminiscences" mentions seeing him in London. In Philadelphia he painted the "Congress Voting Independence" which Edward Savage later added to. This was painted in the "Congress Chamber in the State House," the same room in which the scene portrayed took place and the painting is of great documentary value. The late C. H. Hart wrote a paper upon the subject for the "Pennsylvania Magazine of History."

    1. Bleeker, Leonard. Crayon. Owned by Mrs. E. B. Warfield, New York, 1892.

QUESNAY, ALEXANDER MARIE

Flourished 1784, New York City.
Portrait painter in miniature, portrait draughtsman in crayon, and dancing and drawing teacher.

Numerous extended advertisements inserted in the New York newspapers during 1784 concerning his Academy for Dancing and Drawing are reprinted in W. Kelby: Notes on American Artists.

RAMAGE, John

b. *before 1763, in Ireland;* d. *October 24, 1802, Montreal, Canada.*
Miniature painter.

About twenty-five miniatures by John Ramage have been recorded. For these he invariably made the gold frames himself. He is first heard of attending the Dublin Society Schools in 1763. He worked as an artist and goldsmith in Boston in 1775 and was also a member of the Royal Irish Volunteers. In 1776 he visited Halifax, Nova Scotia. He was with the British troops in New York in 1777, settling shortly on William Street as an artist. In 1794 he went to Canada. See Strickland: Dictionary of Irish Artists.

1. Washington, George. 14½ x 12. Signed: "J. Ramage, March 2d, 1789." Owned by Mr. Robert Fridenberg, N. Y.

ROBERTS, John

b. *1768, Scotland;* d. *1803, New York.*
Engraver, miniature painter, and crayon portrait draughtsman.

He came to America in 1768. He later relinquished art to carry on experiments in steam navigation.

ROBERTSON, Archibald

b. *May 8, 1765, Monymusk, Scotland;* d. *1835, New York.*
Miniature painter.

Ramage — Robertson: 58

ARCHIBALD ROBERTSON was the brother of Alexander Robertson and Andrew Robertson. All three were excellent miniaturists. He came to America in 1791 where he was joined by his brother Alexander in 1792. Together they established a drawing academy in New York. Besides his work in miniature he was also an architect and drew in crayons. His miniature on marble of George Washington is at the New York Historical Society. See "Century Magazine," May, 1890.

ROPES, JOSEPH

b. *1812, Salem, Massachusetts; living in 1879 in New York.*
Crayon portrait draughtsman.

He studied with J. R. Smith and at the National Academy in 1847. From 1855 to 1865 he was in Hartford. From 1865 to 1876 he lived in Italy, settling in the latter year in Philadelphia where he stayed many years. See French: "Art and Artists of Connecticut."

ROWSE, SAMUEL WORCESTER

b. *January 29, 1822, Bath, Maine;* d. *May 24, 1901, Morristown, New Jersey.*
Portrait draughtsman and portrait painter in oils.

After a brief period in Augusta, Maine, as an engraver, Samuel W. Rowse came to Boston in 1852 and worked for a lithographic firm. He soon after established himself as an excellent crayon portrait

Ropes — Rowse: 59

SAINT-MEMIN: RICHARD DOBBS SPAIGHT

*Belonging to and reproduced by the courtesy of The National
Museum, Independence Hall Group, in the Art Collection,
Independence Hall, Philadelphia, Pa.*

draughtsman. He wanted to become an actor but at the end of a few performances in Richard III, deserted the stage on account of his shyness, a trait that gained for him the title of "the silent." However, he made many friends. Thoreau mentions him in his "Journal" for 1854; and references to him are in James Russell Lowell's letters for 1860, 1866 and 1868. He visited the Nortons at Newport. Dr. Edward Waldo Emerson wrote an appreciative account of him in "Early Days of the Saturday Club," to which club Rowse was elected a member in 1864. A pen and ink self portrait of Rowse is reproduced in Dr. Emerson's book. About 1869 or perhaps earlier he undertook painting a few portraits in oils. At the Studio Building where he lived in 1861 and worked for a number of years he had as a friend, Eastman Johnson. In 1872 with his friend Chauncey Wright, he visited London and was frequently the guest of Charles Eliot Norton. While in London he met Ruskin and is recorded as saying, "He wanted me to hold the brush while he painted." About 1880 he moved to New York. In 1881 he visited Paris. With his friend Eastman Johnson he visited London in 1891. He is represented in the large portrait by Eastman Johnson called, "Two Men," now at the Metropolitan Museum and reproduced in the "World's Work," December, 1906. At one time he was in Rome for his health. He finally settled in Morristown, New Jersey, where he died, leaving a considerable estate. His work was in demand regularly and in later years he was some-

Rowse — *Continued:* 60

times paid as much as four hundred dollars for his portrait drawings.

Rowse's portraits are of great excellence. They are drawn in black crayon and although large in size recall in execution the work of the English pencil portrait draughtsman, Samuel Lawrence. An obituary notice of Rowse appeared in the New York "Tribune" for May 26, 1901.

1. Ames, Mrs. Photograph owned by Fogg Art Museum, Harvard.
2. Appleton, F. J. Photograph owned by Fogg Art Museum, Harvard.
3. Appleton, Thomas Gold. (1812-1884.) Drawn 1861. Brother of Mrs. Longfellow.
4. Agassiz, Jean Louis Rodolph. (1807-1873.) Drawn about 1856. Owned by Mrs. Ida H. Higginson, Manchester by the Sea, Massachusetts.
5. Bullard, Louisa (Norton.)
6. Bullard, W. S.
7. Bullard, four portraits of the children of W. S. Bullard. The Bullard portraits all owned by Miss K. E. Bullard, Lenox, Massachusetts.
8. Cheney, John. Charcoal. Drawn 1880. Owned by Mr. F. W. Cheney, 1895.
9. Curtis, Burrill. About 25 x 20. Owned by Mrs. G. W. Curtis, Ashfield, Massachusetts.
10. Curtis, G. W. A photograph owned by Fogg Art Museum, Harvard.
11. Durand, Asher Brown. (1796-1886.) Drawn 1857. Owned by John Durand, 1894.
12. Dwight, Howard. Memorial Hall, Harvard.
13. Emerson, Ralph Waldo. Drawn 1858. Destroyed. Photograph reproduced in Emerson: Journal, v. 6; also E. L. Cary: Emerson, p. 192.
14. Emerson, Ralph Waldo. (1803-1882.) Drawn 1858. Re-

Rowse—*Continued:* 61

produced in Emerson: Journal, v. 6. Owned by Miss Sara Norton, Boston. Also reproduced in E. L. Cary: Emerson, p. 36.

15. Field, James Thomas. (1817-1881.)
16. Field, Kate.
17. Gannett, Reverend Ezra Stiles.
18. Hawthorne, Nathaniel. (1804-1864.) Photograph owned by Fogg Museum, Harvard.
19. Higginson, Cecile Pauline. Drawn about 1871.
20. Longfellow, Henry Wadsworth. (1807-1882.) Drawn 1858. Photograph owned by Fogg Museum, Harvard.
21. Longfellow, Mrs. Henry Wadsworth. Drawn 1859. Reproduced in S. Longfellow: "Life of Longfellow."
22. Lowell, Francis Cabot.
23. Lowell, Mrs. Francis Dunlap.
24. Lowell, James Russell. (1819-1891.) Drawn 1855. Photograph owned by Fogg Museum, Harvard. Engraved by J. A. Wilcox. Owned by Charles E. Norton, 1895.
25. Norton, Charles Elliott. (b. 1827.) Owned by Miss Sara Norton, Boston.
26. Norton, Mrs. Charles Elliott. Drawn 1861. Reproduced in: Letters of C. E. Norton, 1913.
27. Norton, Grace. 25 x 20. Owned by Miss G. Norton, Cambridge, Massachusetts.
28. Norton, Jane. 25 x 20. Owned by Miss G. Norton, Cambridge, Massachusetts.
29. Norton, Susan (Sedgwick.) Owned by Miss Sara Norton, Boston.
30. Putnam, James Lowell. Photograph owned by Fogg Art Museum, Harvard.
31. Shaw, Louis. Drawn 1873.
32. Shaw, Marian, later Mrs. Houghton. Drawn 1873.
33. Shaw, Pauline, later Mrs. Fenno. Drawn 1873.
34. Shaw, Mrs. Pauline Agassiz. Drawn 1873.
35. Shaw, Quincy. Drawn 1873.
36. Shaw, Robert. Drawn 1873.

Rowse — *Continued:* 62

37. Sparks, Mary Crowninshield. Drawn 1875. Reproduced in Adams: Life of Jared Sparks, 1893.

38. Stillman, William James. Drawn 1856. Reproduced in Stillman: Autobiography, 1901.

39. Sturges, Henry K. Owned by Mrs. H. C. Sturgis.

40. Thoreau, Henry David. (1817-1862.) Drawn 1854. Reproduced in Sanborn: Thoreau. Owned by Concord Public Library.

41. Winthrop, Theodore. (1828-1861.) Photograph owned by Fogg Art Museum, Harvard.

SAINT-MÉMIN, CHARLES BALTHAZER JULIEN
FEVRET DE

b. *March 12, 1770, Dijon, France;* d. *there June 23, 1852.*

Portrait engraver and draughtsman.

SAINT-MEMIN came of the lesser French nobility. His father, Benigne-Charles Fevret de Saint-Mémin was a counsellor in the parliament at Dijon. His mother, Victorie-Marie de Notmans came from San Domingo. Young Saint-Mémin was educated first by Abbe Liebaut, then by M. Chiquet, a professor in the College of Dijon and finally at the Military School in Paris, which he entered April 1, 1784. On May 8, 1785 he left the military school with the rank of supernumerary ensign, being promoted to ensign on April 27, 1788. During his student days he had studied art and drew portraits it is said, "with an exactitude perfectly geometrical." He joined the "Army of the Princes" in 1790, ranking as lieutenant colonel. During his leisure while stationed between Coblenz and Cologne he painted miniatures in monochrome on ivory. When the

Saint-Mémin: 63

army was disbanded in 1790 he was discharged with the rank of lieutenant colonel by brevet. In 1793 he was in Switzerland and practiced wood carving. March of the same year he left France with his father to escape the French Revolution, intending to go to the plantations of Madame Saint-Mémin in San Domingo. They travelled by way of Holland, England, Canada and the United States. Upon their arrival in New York they learned of the negro insurrection in San Domingo, so abandoned their plans. His mother and sister then joined them. For a while Saint-Mémin and his father cultivated a vegetable garden. They presently met John R. Livingston who took young Saint-Mémin to a public library where from an encyclopædia the young man taught himself engraving. In 1796 he engraved two views of New York. One of these was drawn from what is now Columbia Heights, Brooklyn. Several other plates are dated 1796. He then commenced engraving the small profile portraits for which he is famous. With a "physionotrace" he traced the exact size profile of the sitter on a sheet of tinted paper and upon the slight foundation made a finished drawing in black and white crayon. This he reduced by means of a pantograph to a disc of copper about two inches in diameter and engraved, charging thirty-three dollars for the drawing, the plate and a dozen proofs. From 1796 to 1798 he was still in New York. He also worked in Burlington, New Jersey, where his mother had started a school. From 1803 to 1807 he was in Washington,

Saint-Mémin — *Continued:* 64

Baltimore, Annapolis, Alexandria, and Georgetown. In 1808 he visited Virginia, staying chiefly
in Norfolk and Richmond. In 1809 he went to
South Carolina where he worked mainly in Charleston. In 1810 he was back in New York. The same
year he revisited France, returning in 1812. At this
time he started painting portraits in oil and landscapes. In October, 1814, he sailed for France
never to return. He settled in Dijon where he was
appointed director of the Museum in 1817, a position he held the rest of his life.

Saint-Mémin had at least two assistants in the
United States. The names of these artists were
Lemet and Valdenuit. Both are listed in the present volume. Another artist whose methods were
identical with those of Saint-Mémin was named
Boudier. He is likewise listed in this volume. Saint-
Mémin ranks as the greatest early American black
crayon portrait draughtsman. This statement is not
minimized by the fact that the profile was traced
with a machine. Only the most general outline
could be obtained in this manner and Saint-Mémin's power is shown in the masterly assurance and
accuracy of his draughtsmanship. Of the two collections of engravings that he kept for himself one
now belongs to the Corcoran Gallery of Art. It
contains about 760 engravings. A photographic fo-
lio of the collection was published by Elias Dexter
in 1862. A biographical introduction translated
from the French is included in this volume. An appreciative article on Saint-Mémin appeared in the

Saint-Mémin — *Continued:* 65

"Brooklyn Museum Quarterly," January, 1918. By some curious oversight William Dunlap did not include Saint-Mémin in his "History of the Arts of Design," published in 1834.

1. Aylett, General Philip. 22 x 16. Owned by Mrs. Hoge, Richmond, Va.
2. Bache, Theophylact. (1734-1807.) Owned by Mr. T. W. Satterthwaite, New York, 1877. Engraved for: Magazine of American History, November, 1877.
3. Bassett, Richard. (d. 1815.) Drawn 1802. Owned by Mr. R. H. Bayard, Baltimore, 1892. Reproduced in C. W. Bowen: Centennial of Inauguration of Washington.
4. Brackett, Major David Watson. Owned by Mr. T. S. Watson, Charlottesville, Va.
5. Burr, Aaron. (1756-1836.) Owned by J. W. Bouton, N. Y., 1887. Reproduced in the Curio, December, 1887.
6. Cabell, Hannah Hemingham, 21¾ x 15¾. Owned by Mr. W. G. Brown, Columbus, Ohio.
7. Cabell, William H. About 19 x 14. Owned by Mr. Isaac Carrington, Richmond.
8. Campbell, James. 21 x 15½. Owned by Mr. H. L. Pratt. Reproduced in J. H. Morgan: Early American Paintings, Brooklyn Museum, 1917.
9. Carroll, Charles. (1737-1832.) Drawn 1804. Owned by Miss E. L. Harper, Baltimore, 1892. Reproduced in C. W. Bowen: "Centennial of Inauguration of Washington."
10. Cleveland, William. (1777-1842.) 21 x 16. Owned by Peabody Museum, Salem, Massachusetts. Reproduced in: Marine Room Peabody Museum, 1921.
11. Clinton, Governor George. (1739-1812.)
12. Clinton, Lady, née Cornelia Tappan. The Clinton portraits both owned by Mrs. Pierre Van Cortlandt, Cortlandt Manor, New York, 1880. See: American Magazine of History, December, 1880.
13. Coale, Mary Abby Willing. (b. 1789.) Drawn about

Saint-Mémin — *Continued:* 66

1809. Owned by the Misses Coale, Baltimore. Reproduced in Morse: Two Centuries of Costume in America.

14. Cocke, James. About 19¾ x 14. Owned by Miss Hoffman, Leesburg, Va.

15. Cox, Mrs., wife of Colonel Cox, Mayor of Georgetown, D. C. Drawn 1804. Owned by Miss Clementina Smith, Washington, D. C., 1922.

16. Custis, Nelly. 5⅜ x 4¼. Owned by Mr. R. T. Haines Halsey. New York, 1922.

17. Decatur, Commodore Stephen. (1779-1820.) Owned by Mr. E. Shippen, Pennsylvania. Reproduced in G. C. Lee: History of North America, v. 12, p. 148.

18. Gamble, Colonel Robert. About 19 x 14. Owned by Mr. Isaac Carrington, Richmond.

19. Giles, General Aquila. 19 x 13¼.

20. Giles, Mrs. Aquila, née Elizabeth Shipton. 19 x 13½. Both Giles portraits reproduced in Catalogue: F. B. Smith Sale, New York, 1920.

21. Gourdin, Theodore. 21½ x 15¾. Owned by Mr. J. H. Morgan. Reproduced in J. H. Morgan: Early American Paintings, Brooklyn Museum, 1917.

22. Harper, Robert Goodloe. Owned by Mrs. W. C. Pennington. Baltimore, Maryland. Reproduced in S. A. Stevens: Albert Gallatin, p. 98.

23. Hastings, Seth. (1762-1831.) 22½ x 17. Owned by Mr. H. L. Pratt. Reproduced in J. H. Morgan: Early American Paintings, Brooklyn Museum, 1917.

24. Herbert Robert Beverly. Drawn 1807. 21 x 15½. Owned by Mr. R. B. Herbert, Columbia, South Carolina, 1921. On loan at the Corcoran Gallery of Art, Washington, D. C.

25. Hill, William, of Wilmington, N. C. About 19¾ x 19. Owned by Mrs. Pilkington, Richmond.

26. Jefferson, Thomas. (1743-1826). Drawn 1805. 18 x 12. Owned by Mr. J. C. Bancroft, Boston, 1893. Reproduced

Saint-Mémin — *Continued: 67*

JAMES SHARPLES: ISAIAH THOMAS

The American Antiquarian Society, Worcester, Mass.

in C. W. Bowen: "Centennial of Inauguration of Washington;" also McClure's Magazine, May, 1898, p. 53.

27. Johnston, Lady, née Livingston. Owned by Mr. Charles A. Munn, N. Y., 1922.

28. Latimer, James, of Philadelphia. 21 x 16½. Owned by Miss Hoffman, Leesburg, Va.

29. Lee, Silas. Owned by Bowdoin College.

30. Lee, Mrs. Silas. Owned by Bowdoin College.

31. Macomb, Alexander. (1782-1841.) Owned by Miss J. S. Dinsmore, 1892. Reproduced in C. W. Bowen: "Centennial of Inauguration of Washington," p. 51.

32. MacHenry, James. Owned by estate of J. H. MacHenry, Pikesville, Maryland. Reproduced in C. W. Ford: Washington, v. 2, p. 235.

33. Marshall, John. (1755-1835.) Drawn 1808. Owned by Mr. T. M. Smith, Baltimore, 1892. Reproduced in C. W. Bowen: Centennial of Inauguration of Washington. Also: Century Magazine, September, 1889.

34. Morris, Captain Samuel. Owned by Miss Anna Morris, 1908. Reproduced in R. C. Moon: Morris Family, Supplement, v. 4, p. 136.

35. Murray, Mary (Dorsey.) Drawn about 1804. Owned by Miss Cheston, West River, Maryland, 1922.

36. Nicholas, Philip Norborne, of Richmond, Va. About 21¼x15½. Owned by Mrs. Carter, Redlands, Charlottesville, Va.

37. Parker, Josiah. Owned by Mr. A. K. Parker, Portsmouth, Virginia, 1892. Reproduced in C. W. Bowen: Centennial of Inauguration of Washington, p. 112.

38. Revere, Paul. (1735-1818.) Drawn 1801. Owned by the Misses Riddle, Hingham, Massachusetts, 1898. Reproduced in E. H. Goss: Paul Revere; also: Scribner's Magazine, January, 1898, p. 12.

39. Rider, Alexander. Owned by Metropolitan Museum.

40. Robertson, Thomas Bolling. Owned by Mr. W. Robertson, Abingdon, Virginia. 1881. See: American Magazine of History, v. 7, p. 297 and 460.

Saint-Mémin — *Continued:* 68

41. Sedgwick, Theodore. (1746-1813.) Drawn 1801. Owned by Mr. H. D. Sedgwick, Stockbridge, Massachusetts, 1892. Reproduced in C. W. Bowen: Centennial of Inauguration of Washington, p. 92.

42. Smith, Alexander. Drawn 1804. Owned by Mr. J. H. Morgan. Reproduced in Brooklyn Museum: Quarterly, January, 1918.

43. Smith, John Addison. Reproduced in: Ancestral Records and Portraits.

44. Smith, Louis, son of General Samuel Smith. 21½ x 15½. Owned by Mrs. Carter, Redlands, Charlottesville, Va.

45. Smith, General Samuel, son of John Smith. About 25⅝ x 15⅞. Owned by Mrs. Carter, Redlands, Charlottesville, Va.

46. Spaight, Richard Dobbs. (1758-1802.) Owned by National Museum, Independence Hall, Pennsylvania. Reproduced in Art in America, June, 1921. Listed as Number 717 in Dexter: Saint-Memin. There called William Spaight.

47. Stanard, Colonel John. 24 x 17½. Owned by Mr. William S. Stanard, Richmond, Va.

48. Swartout, Samuel.

49. Taylor, Colonel Creed. 21½ x 15½.

50. Taylor, Mrs. Creed. About 19 x 13¾. Both the Taylor portraits owned by Miss Ellen Glasgow, Richmond, Va.

51. Tredell, James. Owned by Mr. Charles E. Johnston, Raleigh, North Carolina.

52. Tucker, Thomas Tudor. Drawn 1805. Owned by Mrs. C. B. T. Coleman, Williamsburgh, Virginia, 1892. Reproduced in C. W. Bowen: Centennial of Inauguration of Washington, p. 11.

53. Washington, George. (1732-1799.) Drawn November, 1798. Owned by Mr. J. C. Brevoort, Brooklyn, 1882. This drawing is now lost. Reproduced in E. B. Johnston: Original Portraits of Washington. Engraved by H. B. Hall, 1880. There described as half life size. Reproduced

Saint-Mémin — *Continued:* 69

in: Century Magazine, February, 1892; McClure's Magazine, February, 1898.

54. Washington, William Augustine. Owned in Maryland, 1922.
55. Wheelock, Paul. Owned in Boston, 1921.
56. Wirt, William. (1772-1834.)
57. Wirt, Mrs. William. The Wirt crayon portraits were once both at the Corcoran Gallery of Art according to E. B. Johnston: Original Portraits of Washington, 1881.

PORTRAITS OF INDIANS. The following eight portraits are all owned by the New York Historical Society. The first is reproduced in J. H. Morgan: "Early American Painters, N. Y. Historical Society," 1921. All measure 21½ x 15¼ and are drawn on pink paper.

58. Chief of the Little Osages.
59. Cachasunghia, Osage Warrior.
60. Osage Warrior.
61. Payouska, Chief of the Great Osages.
62. Osage Warrior.
63. Indian of the Iowas of the Missouri.
64. Indian Girl of the Iowas of the Missouri.
65. Delaware Indian.

PORTRAITS OF UNIDENTIFIED SITTERS

66. Philadelphia Gentleman. 22 x 15½. Owned by Mr. R. T. Haines Halsey.
67. Portrait. 22 x 16. Owned by Mrs. Oppenheimer, Richmond.
68. Portrait. 22 x 16. Owned by Mrs. Oppenheimer.
69. Portrait. 22 x 16. Owned by Mr. E. Randolph Williams, Richmond.
70. Portrait. 22 x 16. Owned by Mr. Hugh Nelson, Jr.
71. Portrait. 24 x 19. Owned by Mrs. Coleman, Williamsburg.
72. Portrait. 16 x 14. Owned by Mr. C. Waller, Williamsburg.

Saint-Mémin — *Continued:* 70

73. Portrait. 20⅝ x 14⅝. Owned by Mr. Valentine, Williamsburg.

SAVAGE, EDWARD

b. *November 26, 1761, Princeton, Massachusetts;* d. *there July 6, 1817.*

Engraver and portrait and historical painter.

Savage was at first a goldsmith and started painting about 1789. He began a portrait of Washington in that year. He went to London in 1791, studied engraving and returned in 1794 as a professional engraver. In Philadelphia he had as his assistant, David Edwind and as his apprentice, John Wesley Jarvis. His engraving "Washington and his family," dated 1788 is his best known work. An extended account of Savage by the late C. H. Hart was published in the "Massachusetts Historical Society Proceedings," 1905.

1. Paine, Robert Treat. (1731-1814.) "Drawn and Engraved by J. B. Longacre from a Sketch by Savage."

SCHOENER, J.

Flourished 1821-1827, New England and Reading, Pennsylvania.

Portrait painter in oils and miniature and crayon portrait draughtsman.

He exhibited at the Pennsylvania Academy in 1817.

SHARPLES, FELIX

b. *before 1789, England;* d. *1844, North Carolina.*
Portrait draughtsman in pastel.

Savage—Sharples, F.: 71

He was the elder son of James Sharples. The late Charles H. Hart in writing of the pastel portrait of Hamilton, owned by the New York Historical Society, speaks of it as by "Felix T. Sharples" after the original by his father. See "McClure's Magazine," February, 1897.

SHARPLES, JAMES

b. *1752, Lancashire, England;* d. *February 26, 1811, New York.*
Portrait draughtsman in pastels.

Although he was trained in France for the Roman Catholic priesthood, James Sharples abandoned these studies, returned to England and studied painting. In 1779 he was living in Cambridge. About 1782 he moved to Bath where he taught drawing and here "a young lady of fashion" who was among his pupils became his third wife. In 1783 he was in London. During all these years, 1779 to 1783, he exhibited at the Royal Academy. In 1794 he went to New York. In 1796 he drew his pastel portrait of Washington, which his wife and perhaps his sons frequently copied. His pastel of Tallyrand now in the Sharples Collection at Bristol, England, was probably made at this time. He enjoyed immense popularity and when he died he left an estate of thirty-five thousand dollars.

Sharples was literally a pastel portrait painter. His pastel portraits are small sized on thick gray paper. His colored powders, which he kept in glass bottles he applied with a brush. He made a collec-

Sharples, J.: 72

tion of portraits for himself merely requesting a sitting. Duplicates were generally ordered. He finished a portrait in about two hours and charged fifteen dollars for a profile and twenty for a full face. Dunlap records that Sharples constructed a large family wagon drawn by one horse and travelled about the country with his family, painting his pastel portraits in many cities.

The pastel portraits of Sharples are of great beauty and accuracy. They recall the work of the French profile draughtsmen and engravers which Sharples must have seen as a youth in France. The dates of the various members of the Sharples family are taken from Mr. Herbert Quick's "Sharples Collection, Bristol Art Gallery." Mr. Quick's information is taken from the Clifton Parish Churchyard. The name is sometimes spelled "Sharpless." The artist's signature to his will in the New York Surrogate's Office, however, gives only one "s."

The "Memorials of Washington" by James Walter published in New York in 1887 are, on the testimony of the eminent historian Parkman, largely forgeries. The book contains reproductions of portraits in oils of Washington and other eminent men said to be painted by Sharples. The result of Parkman's investigation was printed as "Report on the alleged Sharples portraits of Washington," in the Massachusetts Historical Society Proceedings, 2d series, January, 1887, volume 3. A notice of Sharples' death appeared in the Public Advertiser, February 28, 1811: "Died on Tuesday morning at 6

Sharples, J. — *Continued:* 73

o'clock, James Sharples, Esq., in the 59th year of his age. His friends and acquaintances are invited to attend his funeral, from his late dwelling, No. 3 Lispenard Street, upper end of Church Street, this afternoon at 4 o'clock."

1. Adams, John. (1735-1826.) President of United States. Reproduced in Dunlap: History, 1918 edition; also G. C. Lee: History of North America, v. 7, p. 341; also C. W. Bowen: Centennial of Inauguration of Washington, p. 89.
2. Adet, Pierre Auguste. (1763-1832.) French diplomatist. Reproduced in G. C. Lee: History of North America, v. 7, p. 305.
3. Ames, Fisher. (1758-1808.) Statesman. Reproduced in C. W. Bowen: Centennial of Inauguration of Washington, p. 89; also G. C. Lee: History of North America, v. 7, p. 220.
4. Bard, John. (1716-1799.) Physician. Engraved by Leney.
5. Brown, Charles Brockden. (1771-1810.) Novelist. Reproduced in Art in America, 1923.
6. Burr, Aaron. (1756-1836.) Lawyer and statesman. Reproduced in G. C. Lee: History of North America, v. 8, p. 256.
7. Clinton, De Witt. (1769-1828.) Governor of New York. Reproduced in G. C. Lee: History of North America. v. 4, p. 367.
8. Clinton, James. (1736-1812.) General. Reproduced in G. C. Lee: History of North America, v. 4, p. 464.
9. Cruger, Henry. (1739-1827.) Politician.
10. Cushing, Mrs. William, wife of the Justice of the Supreme Court. Reproduced in Dunlap: History of the Arts of Design, 1918 edition.
11. Dayton, Elias. (1737-1807.) Revolutionary Officer.
12. Few, William. (1748-1828.) Soldier.
13. Gates, Horatio. (1728-1806.) Revolutionary Officer. Re-

Sharples, J.—*Continued:* 74

produced in G. C. Lee: History of North America, v. 6, p. 293; also in Art in America and Elsewhere, 1923.

14. Green, Ashbel. (1762-1848.) Clergyman.
15. Hamilton, Alexander. (1757-1804.) Reproduced in G. C. Lee: History of North America, v. 8, p. 256.
16. Hobart, John Sloss. (1738-1805.) Jurist.
17. Jefferson, Thomas. (1743-1826.) President of the United States, 1801-1809. Reproduced in G. C. Lee: History of North America, v. 7, p. 368; also C. W. Bowen: Centennial of Inauguration of Washington, p. 21.
18. Johnson, William Samuel. (1727-1819.)
19. Kent, James. (1763-1847.) Jurist. Reproduced in G. C. Lee: History of North America, v. 12, p. 293.
20. LeFevre, aide to Colonel La Rouerie.
21. Langdon, John. (1739-1819.) Reproduced in G. C. Lee: History of North America, v. 7, p. 93.
22. Laurens, Henry. (1724-1792.) Statesman.
23. Livingston, Robert R. (1746-1813.) Statesman and jurist. Reproduced in C. W. Bowen: Centennial of Inauguration of Washington, p. 45.
24. McHenry, James. (1753-1816.) Reproduced in G. C. Lee: History of North America, v. 6, p. 224.
25. McKean, Thomas. (1734-1817.) Politician and jurist.
26. Madison, Mrs. James née Dorothy Payne. (1772-1849.) Reproduced in C. W. Bowen: Centennial of Inauguration of Washington, p. 258; also in G. C. Lee: History of North America, v. 12, p. 49.
27. Monroe, James. (1758-1831.) President of United States, 1817-25. Reproduced in C. W. Bowen: Centennial of Inauguration of Washington, p. 108.
28. Pinckney, Charles Cotesworth. (1746-1825.) Soldier and Statesman.
29. Putnam, Rufus. (1738-1824.) Soldier.
30. Rush, Dr. Benjamin. (1745-1813.) Reproduced in G. C. Lee: History of North America, v. 6, p. 45.
31. Sherbourne, Colonel Henry. Treasurer of R. I., 1792-1818.

Sharples, J.—*Continued:* 75

JAMES SHARPLES: CHARLES BROCKDEN BROWN

Art Collection, Independence Hall, Philadelphia, Penna. Courtesy of the National Museum Independence Hall Group

32. Smith, Isaac. (1736-1807.) Patriot.
33. Smith, Samuel. (1752-1839.)
34. Smith, William Laughton. (d. 1812.) Diplomatist.
35. Spaight, Richard Dobbs. (1758-1802.) Governor of North Carolina. Reproduced in G. C. Lee: History of North America, v. 7, p. 76.
36. Stoughton, William. Spanish Minister to the United States.
37. Van Berckel. Dutch Minister to U. S.
38. Van Cortlandt, Philip. (1749-1831.) American Soldier. Reproduced in G. C. Lee: History of North America, p. 293.
39. Wadsworth, Jeremiah. (1762-1829.) Jurist. Nephew of George Washington.
40. Washington, Bushrod. (1762-1829.) Jurist. Nephew of George Washington.
41. Washington, George. (1732-1799.) 10 x 8. Drawn in 1796. Reproduced in G. C. Lee: History of North America, v. 6, p. 3; also McClure's Magazine, February, 1897.
42. Wayne, General Anthony. (1745-1796.) Hero of Stony Point.
43. Webster, Noah. (1758-1843.) Philologist.
44. Wilkinson, James. (1757-1825.) General and Politician. Reproduced in G. C. Lee: History of North America, v. 12, p. 108.
45. Yrujo, Don Carlos Marquis de. (1763; d. after 1804.) Spanish diplomat. Reproduction in G. C. Lee: History of North America, v. 7, p. 305.

The foregoing forty-five pastel portraits are in the National Museum, Independence Hall, Philadelphia.

The following note was addressed to the writer by Mr. Wilfred Jordan, Curator, Independence Hall:

"Might I suggest to you that in your note under our list of 45, which appears in the proof, you make some

Sharples, J. — *Continued:* 76

mention of the fact that we in Independence Hall doubt in some cases the attributions given some of our portraits as listed and catalogued here for years. For example, I am convinced that our John Adams is not Adams at all; who it is I cannot say. The same applies to Hamilton and others. In the case of Hamilton I doubt its being a Sharples at all or even the work of anyone of his family. For this reason we have refrained from labeling any of the collection since having the frames done up, only using a key label on the walls of the Sharples room which clearly points out the fact that some of the subjects are in doubt. I simply give you these facts to use as you may see fit."

46. Benson, Egbert. Fullface. Owned by Mr. Charles A. Munn, N. Y., 1922.

47. Borland, Euclid. 10 x 8.

48. Borland, Harriet Godwin, wife of Dr. Borland. 10 x 8.

49. Borland, Roscius Cicero. 10 x 8.

50. Borland, Dr. Thomas Wood. 10 x 8. All the Borland portraits owned by Mrs. T. Borland, Norfolk, Virginia.

51. Braxton, Carter Moore. 8½ x 6½.

52. Braxton, Mrs. Carter Moore, née Anna T. Muse. Both this portrait and the foregoing owned by the Misses Braxton, Fredericksburg, Virginia.

53. Brown, Charles Brockden. (1771-1810.) Novelist. 9½ x 7½. Owned by Worcester Art Museum.

54. Brown, John. (1757-1837.) Member from Virginia to First Congress. Owned by Mrs. W. T. Scott, Frankfort, Kentucky, 1892. Reproduced in C. W. Bowen: Centennial of Inauguration of Washington, p. 119. Owned by Miss Mary M. Scott, Frankfort, Kentucky, 1922.

55. Custis, Eleanor Parke, later Mrs. Lawrence Lewis. Owned by Professor R. B. Winder, Baltimore, 1892. Reproduced in C. W. Bowen: Centennial of Inauguration of Washington, p. 256.

Sharples, J. — *Continued:* 77

56. Custis, George Washington Parke. (1781-1857.) Oval. 9¼ x 7¼. Owned by Washington and Lee University, Lexington, Virginia.

57. Gallatin, Albert. (1776-1849.) 9⅜ x 7⅜. Owned by Metropolitan Museum, New York.

58. Godwin, George. 10 x 8.

59. Godwin, Jeremiah. 10 x 8.

60. Godwin, Sally Wilkinson, wife of Jeremiah. 10 x 8. All the Godwin portraits owned by Mrs. T. Borland, Norfolk, Virginia.

61. Green, Fannie. 10 x 8.

62. Green, Mary Giles. 10 x 8. Both the Green portraits owned by Mrs. T. Borland, Norfolk, Virginia.

63. Griffith, Mrs. Robert Eglesfield. 9 x 7⅝. Owned by Mrs. G. Carter, Leesburg, Virginia.

64. Hamilton, Alexander. (1757-1804.) 9½ x 7½. Owned by New York Historical Society. Reproduced in J. H. Morgan: Early American Painters, New York Historical Society, 1921. The late Charles H. Hart considered this a copy by Felix Sharples. See McClure's Magazine, April, 1897, p. 512.

65. Hamilton, Alexander. (1757-1804.) Drawn 1796. Owned at Manor Hall, Yonkers, New York.

66. Hamilton, Alexander. (1757-1804.) Profile. Owned by Mr. Charles A. Munn, N. Y., 1922.

67. Hamilton, Alexander. (1757-1804.) 8 x 6. Drawn 1796. Owned by Dr. A. M. Hamilton, New York, 1892. Reproduced in C. W. Bowen: Centennial of Inauguration of Washington, p. 26; McClure's Magazine, April, 1897, p. 512.

68. Ingersoll, Josiah. (1763-1839.) 9⅞ x 7⅞. Owned by Metropolitan Museum, New York.

69. Israel, Mrs. Israel née Hannah Erwin. (1758-1814.) Owned by the Ehrich Galleries.

70. Lafayette, Marie Jean Paul Roch Yoes Gilbert Motier Marquis de. (1757-1834.) Soldier and statesman. 10x8. Stan. V. Henkels Sale, December, 1920.

Sharples, J.—*Continued:* 78

71. Langdon, John. Owned by Mr. J. Erving, New York, 1892. Reproduced in C. W. Bowen: Centennial of Inauguration of Washington, p. 105.
72. Livermore, Samuel. Owned by Mr. C. G. Saunders, Lawrence, Massachusetts, 1892. Reproduced in C. W. Bowen: Centennial of Inauguration of Washington, p. 105.
73. Livingston, Robert R. (1746-1813.) 9 x 7. Owned by Mrs. E. F. O. Nelson, 1908.
74. Martin, Alexander. (1740-1807.) Reproduced in A. Henderson: Conquest of Old Southwest.
75. Mason, (?), John (?). 10 x 8. Stan V. Henkels sale, Pennsylvania, December, 1920.
76. Mason, Thomas of Rasberry Plain, Virginia. 9½ x 7½. Owned by C. M. Sparrow, University of Virginia.
77. McClurg, James. (1747-1823.) Oval. 10 x 8. Owned by Ehrich Galleries, 1918. Reproduced in Ehrich Galleries: Hundred Early American Paintings.
78. Mitchell, Samuel L. (1764-1831.) 9 x 7. Owned by New York Historical Society.
79. Morris, Governor. (Perhaps.) Fullface. Owned by Mr. Charles A. Munn, N. Y., 1922.
80. Nicholson, Mrs. Lemuel, née Charlotte Tabb. Drawn 1800. 10 x 8. Owned by Mr. J. H. Morgan. Reproduced in J. H. Morgan: Early American Paintings, Brooklyn Museum, 1917.
81. Parramore, Mrs. Thomas, née Emory Tabb. 10 x 8. Drawn about 1800. Owned by J. H. Morgan. Reproduced in J. H. Morgan: Early American Paintings, Brooklyn Museum, 1917.
82. Patterson, Captain John. 9¼ x 6⅝.
83. Patterson, Mrs. John. Both Patterson portraits owned by Mrs. P. E. Yeatman, Norfolk, Virginia.
84. Robinson, Miss. 9 x 7. Owned by Mrs. Picot, Richmond, Virginia.
85. Skyrin, John. 9½ x 7½. Owned by Mrs. Picot, Richmond, Virginia.

Sharples, J. — *Continued:* 79

86. Smith, Armistead. 9⅛ x 6¾. Owned by Mrs. I. Carrington, Richmond, Virginia.
87. Smith, Elihu. (1771-1798.) Drawn about 1795-97. 10x8. Owned by Mr. W. H. Crittenden, 1917. Reproduced in J. H. Morgan: Early American Paintings, Brooklyn Museum, 1917.
88. Smith, Elihu. (1771-1798.) Owned by New York Historical Society.
89. Smith, Dr. Reuben. 10 x 8. Drawn about 1795-97.
90. Smith, Dr. Reuben. 10 x 8. Drawn about 1795-97, at Litchfield, Connecticut. Owned by Mr. Witt Crittendon, 1917. Reproduced in J. H. Morgan: Early American Paintings, Brooklyn Museum, 1917.
91. Smith, William Patterson. 10 x 8. Owned by Mrs. I. Carrington, Richmond, Virginia.
92. Strobel, Mrs. Daniel. Crayon.
93. Temple, Benjamin. 9 x 7. Owned by Miss L. Temple, Richmond, Virginia.
94. Temple, Mrs. Benjamin. 9 x 7. Owned by Miss L. Temple, Richmond, Virginia.
95. Temple, Sir John. Drawn about 1796. Owned by Mr. R. C. Winthrop, 1892.
96. Temple, Lady. Drawn about 1796. Owned by Mr. R. C. Winthrop, 1892.
97. Thomas, Isiah. (1749-1831.) Owned by American Antiquarian Society, Worcester. Reproduced in: Proceedings of the American Antiquarian Society, October, 1920.
98. Todd, Sarah Virginia. 9 x 7. Owned by Mrs. Lightfoot, Richmond, Virginia.
99. Tompkins, Mrs. Christopher. 9 x 7. Owned by Mrs. P. E. Yeatman, Norfolk, Virginia.
100. Tyler, John. Aged 25 years.
101. Wadsworth, Jeremiah. Owned by Mr. C. A. Brinley, Philadelphia, 1892. Reproduced in C. W. Bowen: Centennial of Inauguration of Washington, p. 80.
102. Washington, George. Drawn 1798. Owned by General

Sharples, J.—*Continued:* 80
79

G. W. C. Lee, Lexington, Virginia, 1892. Reproduced in E. B. Johnston: Original Portraits of Washington.

103. Washington, George. Owned by Mr. Charles A. Munn, N. Y., 1922.

104. Washington, George. Drawn 1796. Owned at Manor Hall, Yonkers, New York.

105. Washington, George. Owned by David Hoffman, 1881.

106. Washington, George. Owned by Honorable James Hillhouse, New Haven, Connecticut, before 1881.

107. Washington, George. Drawn for Judge Peters.

108. Washington, George. Owned by Mrs. Morton Lewis, Bridgewater, Pennsylvania, 1881.

109. Washington, George. 9 x 7. Owned by Mr. H. L. Pratt. Reproduced in J. H. Morgan: Early American Paintings, Brooklyn Museum, 1917.

110. Washington, George. Owned by Wadsworth Athenaeum, Hartford, Connecticut.

111. Washington, George. 10 x 7¾. Formerly in Lord Belper's Collection. Owned by Mr. J. P. Morgan. Reproduced in J. H. Morgan. Early American Paintings, Brooklyn Museum, 1917.

112. Washington, George. Owned by the Sons of the Revolution. Reproduced in color in H. P. Johnston: Memoir of Benjamin Tallmadge.

113. Washington, Martha. Owned by Wadsworth Athenaeum, Hartford, Connecticut.

114. Webster, Noah. (1758-1843.) Full face. Owned by Mr. Charles A. Munn, N. Y., 1922.

115. Winder, Comfort Gore. 9½ x 7½.

116. Winder, Dr. John. 9½ x 7½.

117. Winder, John Harmonson. 9½ x 7½.

118. Winder, Mary Harmonson. 9½ x 7½. All the Winder portraits owned by the Misses Garrett, Williamsburg, Virginia.

119. Portrait of a man. 9 x 7. Owned by Mr. Herbert L. Pratt.

120. Portrait of a man. 9½ x 7½. Owned by Ehrich Galleries.

Sharples, J.—*Continued:* 81

JAMES SHARPLES: GEORGE WASHINGTON

The Wadsworth Athenaeum, Hartford, Ct.

121. Portrait of a man. 10 x 8. F. Bulkeley Smith Collection, 1920.

The following fifty-seven pastel portraits by James Sharples are in the Bristol Art Gallery at Bristol, England. The expression "three-quarters" means the face is turned three-quarters.

122. Adams, John. (1735-1876.) Three-quarters to left.
123. Banks, Sir. Joseph. (1743-1820.) Naturalist. Three-quarters to left.
124. Beaujolais, Count de. (1799-1808.) Brother of Louis Philippe. Three-quarters to right.
125. Beddoes, Dr. Thomas. (1760-1808.) Scientist. Three-quarters to right.
126. Bilsborough, Dr. Three-quarters to right.
127. Brown, Charles Brockden. (1771-1810.) Three-quarters to right.
128. Brown, Mrs. Profile to left.
129. Browne, Arthur M. (1756-1805.) Profile to left. Possibly Mrs. Sharples.
130. Burr, Aaron. (1756-1836.) Profile to left.
131. Bush, Miss. Profile to left.
132. Cogan, Dr. Thomas. (1736-1818.) Philosopher. Three-quarters to right. Drawn December, 1803.
133. Darwin, Dr. Erasmus. (1731-1802.) Naturalist. Three-quarters to left.
134. Davy, Sir Humphrey. (1778-1829.) Chemist. Three-quarters to left.
135. Dunbar, Sir G. Profile to left.
136. Fisher, Myers. Well-known Quaker. Three-quarters to left.
137. Gallatin, Albert. (1761-1849.) Financier. Profile to left.
138. Godwin, William. (1756-1836.) Political writer. Profile to left.
139. Greaves, Rev. Richard. (1745-1804.) Profile to left.
140. Hamilton, Alexander. (1757-1804.) Profile to left.

Sharples, J. — *Continued:* 82

141. Haygarth, Dr. (1740-1827.) Profile to left.
142. Herschel, Sir William. (1738-1822.) Astronomer. Profile to left.
143. Hill, Rev. Rowland. (1744-1833.) Profile to left.
144. Jackson, Francis J. (1770-1814.) British Diplomat. Three-quarters to right. Drawn March, 1810.
145. Jackson, Mrs. Frances J. Three-quarters to left. Drawn March, 1810.
146. Jefferson, Thomas. (1743-1826.) Profile to left.
147. Johnson, Dr. of Derby. Three-quarters to left.
148. King, Dr. John. Three-quarters to left.
149. La Fayette (?), Monsieur (?). Profile to left.
150. La Roche Fancould-Liancourt, Duke de. (1747-1827.) French Philanthropist. Profile to left.
151. Law, Thomas. (1759-1834.) Profile to left.
152. Liston, Sir Robert. (1742-1836.) Profile to left.
153. Liston, Lady. Profile to right.
154. Madison, James. (1751-1836.) Three-quarters to left.
155. Madison, Mrs. James. (1772-1849.) Profile to left.
156. Montpensier, Duke de. (1775-1807.) Brother of Louis Phillippe. Three-quarters to right.
157. Moore, Clement Clarke. (1779-1863.) Three-quarters to left. Drawn March, 1810.
158. Morgan, Mrs.
159. Morris, Governeur. (1752-1816.) Slightly turned to left.
160. Morse, Rev. Jedediah. (1761-1826.) Profile to left.
161. North, General William. (1735-1836.) Aide to von Steuben. Three-quarters to right.
162. Philippe, Louis. (1773-1850.) King of France. Three-quarters to left.
163. Priestley, Dr. Joseph. (1733-1804.) Three-quarters to right. Copy by Mrs. Sharples in National Portrait Gallery, London.
164. Rush, Dr. Benjamin. (1745-1813.) Profile to left.
165. Southey, Robert. (1774-1843.) Poet. Profile to left.
166. Stewart, John. (1749-1822.) Philosopher. Three-quarters to right.

Sharples, J.— *Continued:* 83

167. Strutt, William. (1756-1830.) Inventor. Three quarters to right.
168. Talleyrand, Charles Maurice de. (1754-1838.) Three-quarters to left.
169. Temple, Mr. Three-quarters to left.
170. Thouisy, Commander de. Three-quarters to left.
171. Townsend, Charles. Wax portrait miniaturist.
172. Vanderhorst, Mr. Turned slightly to left.
173. Washington, George. (1732-1799.) 9 x 7. Three-quarters to right.
174. Washington, George. (1732-1799.) Profile to left.
175. Washington, Martha. (1732-1802.) Profile to left.
176. Watson, Rev. Richard. (1737-1816.) Three-quarters to left.
177. Wilmot, Lady. Three-quarters to right.
178. Unknown. Naval officer. Three-quarters to left.

SHARPLES, Mrs. James (Ellen)

b. *March 4, 1769, Birmingham, England;* d. *March 4, 1849, Bristol, England.*
Portrait draughtsman in pastel.

Mrs. Sharples frequently copied her husband's portraits very faithfully in the exact size. After her husband's death she returned to England and settled in Bristol. In 1845 she gave two thousand pounds for the founding of the Bristol Fine Arts Academy. In her will she left in 1849 three thousand four hundred and sixty-five pounds more. At this institution there is today the "Sharples Collection" of ninety-seven pictures by her husband, herself, James Junior and Rolinda. Her daughter Rolinda (1794-1838), was born in New York but none of her paintings were made in this country. See:

Sharples, Mrs. J. (E.) : 84

83

"Century Magazine," February, 1894. Also "Magazine of American History," v. 11, p. 513.

1. Washington, George. Full face. Attributed to Mrs. Sharples. Owned by Mr. Charles A. Munn, N. Y., 1922.

SHARPLES, JAMES, JR.

b. *1789, England; d. August 10, 1839, Bristol, England.*

Portrait draughtsman in pastel.

The younger son of James Sharples. He frequently copied his father's work. He returned to England with his mother and sister after his father's death.

SHINDLER, A. ZENO

Flourished 1855-1860, Philadelphia.

Portrait draughtsman in crayons.

STAIGG, RICHARD MORRELL

b. *September 7, 1817, Leeds, England; d. October 11, 1881, Newport, Rhode Island.*

Portrait painter in oils and miniature and portrait draughtsman in crayons.

RICHARD M. STAIGG or Stagg, as the name is sometimes spelled, worked in an architect's office in England before coming to the United States in 1831, when he settled at Newport. His early work is entirely in miniature. He was elected N. A. in 1861. He visited Europe in 1867-1869 and 1872-1874. He spent his last years in Newport. See Tuckerman: "Book of Artists." Tuckerman speaks of a "series

Sharples, J., Jr. — Staigg: 85

PORTRAIT OF HIMSELF
BY GILBERT STUART
After the etched copy by Falconer

of crayon heads of children remarkable for delicate accuracy and truth."

> 1. Dumaresq, Captain Philip. Drawn 1847. Crayon. Reproduced in S. E. Morrison: Maritime History of Massachusetts.

STORY, WILLIAM WETMORE

b. *February 12, 1815, Salem, Massachusetts;* d. *October 7, 1895, Vallambrosa, Italy.*
Sculptor and author.

Graduated from Harvard in 1838, studied law with his father, Joseph Story the eminent jurist, wrote several law books, then finally became an artist in 1848 and went to Italy where he lived for the most part the rest of his life. The late Henry James wrote his biography.

> 1. Story, Joseph. Crayon. Drawn from memory in 1851. Owned by Mr. F. H. Story, Boston, 1900. Engraved by J. Cheney for Longacre: National Portrait Gallery. Reproduced in A. B. Magruder: John Marshall, p. 58. Engraving reproduced in: Writings and Speeches of Webster, v. 3, p. 298.

STUART, GILBERT

b. *December 3, 1755, near Kingston, Rhode Island;* d. *July 9, 1828, Boston.*
Eminent American portrait painter.

As a boy Gilbert Stuart received slight assistance from Cosmo Alexander, a Scotchman who visited Rhode Island. He fortunately started early in life at his profession. From 1773 to 1774 he was in Edinburgh; from 1774 until the eve of the Revolution he was in Newport. Immediately before the first gun shots of Bunker's Hill he left the country in 1775, and went to London. He earned his living as an organist for about two years, then sought West's assistance, and finally started independently as a portrait painter. From 1788 to 1793 he was in Dublin, leaving the latter year for Philadelphia to avoid debt. A few years later he painted the famous portraits of George Washington. He moved to Washington in 1803, and to Boston in 1806. Two portrait drawings by Gilbert Stuart have been described. One is a rapid line drawing in ink of himself reproduced in Mason's "Life of Stuart." The other is a crayon drawing of Thomas Jefferson in profile. He painted a monochrome of Jefferson in 1805. Jefferson wrote to Joseph Delaplaine in 1813 that it was in "water color." In 1819 he wrote to General Dearborn, that this was a profile portrait "on paper with crayon." In his letter to Stuart, written earlier, Jefferson speaks of two portraits, one of which Stuart wanted to keep and have engraved, the other to go to Jefferson himself. See "McClure's Magazine," May, 1898. There is a crayon profile of Thomas Jefferson "supposed to be one of eight made by Gilbert Stuart, bought at sale of Walleck, the actor" that is owned by Colonel A. D. Martin, Frankfort, Kentucky, 1922.

SULLY, ROBERT MATTHEW
  b. *July 17, 1803, Petersburg, Va.;* d. *October 16, 1855, Madison, Wisconsin.*
  Portrait Painter.
      Nephew of Thomas Sully. Studied with his uncle
                                          Sully, R. M.: 87

during his youth and later in England during 1824-1826.

1. Randolph, John, of Roanoke. Pen and ink sketch. Signed: "R. M. Sully, 1835." Owned by Mr. Robert Fridenberg, N. Y.

SULLY, THOMAS

b. *June, 1783, Horncastle, England;* d. *November 5, 1872, Philadelphia.*
Portrait painter in oils and miniature.

The parents of Thomas Sully were English actors who moved with their family to Charleston, South Carolina in 1792. He was first employed in an insurance office but neglecting his work he was allowed to study art with a French miniature painter who was an uncle by marriage. The pupil and teacher came to blows after a short time and young Thomas sailed for Norfolk where he joined his brother Lawrence in 1801. His brother was also a miniature painter and together they painted both in Norfolk and Richmond. When his brother died he married his widow. In 1806 he went to New York where he received assistance from Jarvis and in 1801 he moved to Boston to study under Stuart. He was again in New York in 1808. In 1809 he was in Philadelphia. During 1809-1810 he studied in London, returning to Philadelphia in the spring of the latter year. From then on Philadelphia remained his permanent home although he made frequent visits to all the principal cities. He revisited London in 1837 to paint the portrait of Queen Victoria. See E. Biddle and M. Fielding: "Thomas

Sully, T.: 88

Sully" the authoritative volume on the artist, listing over two thousand of his portraits.

1. Adams, John Quincy. (1767-1848.) Chalk study to finish the whole length left unfinished by Gilbert Stuart. Drawn 1829. (Biddle and Fielding No. 5.)
2. Brown, Jacob. (1775-1828.) Drawing made for the Congressional Medal Design, September, 1817. 6 x 6. (Biddle and Fielding No. 209.)
3. Gaines, Edward Pendleton. (1777-1849. Drawing made for the Congressional Medal Design, September, 1817. 6 x 6. (Biddle and Fielding, No. 630.)
4. Jackson, General Andrew. (1767-1845.) Drawn January, 1815. Black crayon on blue paper. About life size. Inscribed "General Andrew Jackson taken immediately after the Battle of New Orleans. T. Sully." Owned by Mrs. A. Sully, Brooklyn, New York, 1922.
5. McComb, General Alexander. (1782-1841.) Drawn for the Congressional Medal Design, September, 1817. 6 x 6. (Biddle and Fielding, No. 1178.)
6. Miller, General James. (1776-1851.) Drawn for the Congressional medal Design, September, 1817. 6 x 6. (Biddle and Fielding, No. 1244.)
7. Porter, David. (1780-1843.) Drawn for the Congressional Medal Design, September, 1817. 6 x 6. (Biddle and Fielding, No. 1400.)
8. Ripley, General James W. (1794-1870.) Drawn for the Congressional Medal Design, September, 1817. 6 x 6. (Biddle and Fielding, No. 1477.)
9. Scott, General Winfield. (1786-1866.) Drawn for the Congressional Medal Design, September, 1817. 6 x 6. (Biddle and Fielding, No. 1559.)
10. Stewart, Commodore Charles. Pencil sketch from life for Congressional Medal. Owned by Mr. Earl W. Huckel, Germantown, Pennsylvania, 1922.
11. Sully, Jane Cooper. Pastel. Owned by Mr. H. H. Smith, 1921.

Sully, T. — *Continued:* 89

12. Sully, Sarah and Jane. Drawn New York, 1806. Ink and crayon. Owned by Mr. Andre E. Rueff, Brooklyn, New York.

13. Sully, Thomas. (1783-1872.) Self portrait in pencil. Drawn 1823. Owned by Mr. Charles A. Munn, New York. (Biddle and Fielding, No. 1732.)

THORNTON, WILLIAM

b. *May 27, 1761, Island of Jost Van Dyke, West Indies;* d. *March 28, 1828, Washington, D. C.*

Physician, architect, engraver, and portrait painter in oils and miniature.

DR. THORNTON was of Quaker parentage. He studied medicine in Edinburgh but was also an accomplished artist and architect. From 1781 to 1783 he was in England and Scotland. In the former year he engraved a few plates in mezzo tint. The latter year he came to the United States. He designed the Philadelphia Library building erected in 1790. He was commissioner of public buildings in Washington, D. C., and drew the first plans for the United States Capitol building. He also assisted Thomas Jefferson with the plans for the University of Virginia buildings. The best account of him is to be found in a paper by Mr. A. C. Clark in the "Records of the Columbia Historical Society," Washington, D. C., 1915. A collection of his manuscripts including personal notes is at the Library of Congress. Dr. Thornton copied the profile crayon drawing that Gilbert Stuart made of Jefferson in "Swiss Crayon." See: "McClure's Magazine," May, 1898.

Thornton: 90

TRUMBULL, John

b. *June 6, 1756, Lebanon, Connecticut;* d. *November 10, 1843, New York.*
Historical and portrait painter in oils.

TRUMBULL graduated from Harvard in 1773. In 1775 he became an adjutant in the army under General Gates. He was stationed at Roxbury during the Battle of Bunker's Hill and served later at Crown Point and Ticonderoga. He was also with Washington in New Jersey. In 1777 he resigned his commission, paid a brief visit to Lebanon and then went to Boston to study the paintings of Copley. Bent on improvement he sailed for France in 1780 and then went to London for instruction under West. He was soon arrested as a retaliatory measure for the taking of Major André and was sent to prison. He was released through the intercession of West. In 1782 he returned to Boston. The winter of 1782-83 he kept a store at New Windsor. In 1784 he again went to London to continue his studies. The next year he first planned the series of historical compositions for which he is now famous. The first of these was the Battle of Bunker's Hill. He visited France in 1786 and 1789 and during the latter year witnessed the fall of the Bastile. He then returned to America and made many trips both north and south to paint small oil portraits of the men who took part in the scenes he wished to portray. These portraits, nearly all of them painted on wood about three by four inches, constitute his best work. Many are in the Trum-

Trumbull: 91

bull collection at Yale. In May, 1794, he was appointed secretary to John Jay and sailed for England. During his vacation he worked industriously at his compositions. Goethe saw and admired the "Battle of Bunker's Hill" at Stuttgart where the engraver Müller was making a plate from the picture. The autumn of 1797 Trumbull went to Stuttgart to see the engraver and get the small painting. He was detained in Paris on his way to London for lack of a passport. He gives a vivid description in his "Autobiography," which deserves reprinting, of Louis David's eloquent intercession in his behalf before Talleyrand. This obtained the required passport and Trumbull returned to London. He revisited the United States during 1804-1806. He left London in 1812 and settled in New York. He became president of the American Academy of Fine Arts in 1816. In exchange for his collection of pictures, Yale University granted him an annuity.

Trumbull's small portraits drawn with a sharp pencil point are of great artistic and documentary value. The time and place they were drawn is generally carefully noted upon the reverse of the portraits. Six pencil portraits of Indian chieftains by Trumbull are owned by Mr. Charles A. Munn.

1. Hopkins, Stephen. (1707-1785.) Owned by Mr. Charles A. Munn, N. Y., 1922.
2. Putnam, Israel. (1718-1790.) Pencil. Engraved by W. Humphreys for Longacre: National Portrait Gallery.
3. Tallmadge, Benjamin. (1754-1835.) Pencil. Engraved for "American Magazine of History," February, 1882. Reproduced in H. P. Johnston: Memoir of Col. Benjamin Tallmadge.

Trumbull—*Continued:* 92

4. Wayne, Anthony. (1745-1796.) Pencil. Engraved by Prud'homme after Herring's copy for Longacre: National Portrait Gallery.
5. Wayne, Anthony. (1745-1796.) Pencil. Owned by Mr. Charles A. Munn, N. Y., 1922.

The following portraits in pencil by Trumbull constituted the "Silliman Collection." They were sold a number of years ago in Philadelphia by Stan. V. Henkels. The catalogue of the sale contains several reproductions after the pencil portraits.

1. Chase, Samuel. (1741-1811.) 5 x 3⅛. Endorsed: "Sam'l Chase Maryland." Owned by Mr. Hall Parker McCullough, 1922.
2. Ellery, William. (1727-1820.) 5 x 3⅛. Endorsed:"Wm. Ellery, Newport, 30 April, 1791." Owned by Mr. Albert Rosenthal, Pa., 1922.
3. Gates, General Horatio. (1728-1806.) 4½ x 3. Endorsed.
4. Glover, Brigadier General. 5 x 4. Endorsed: "B. Gen. Glover, Marblehead, November 13, 1794." Owned by Mr. Hall Parke McCullough, 1922.
5. Greene, Nathaniel. (1742-1786.) 4¾ x 3. Owned by Mr. Hall Parke McCullough, 1922.
6. Hancock, John. 5 x 3¾. Endorsed: "Governor Hancock, Boston, November 25, 1790." Owned by Mr. J. F. Sabin, 1922.
7. Hopkins, John. 5x3⅛. Endorsed: "Jno. Hopkins, 1796."
8. Howard, Colonel John Eager. 5 x 3$\frac{1}{16}$. Owned by Mr. Albert Rosenthal, Pa., 1922.
9. Mercer, Hugh. (1721-1777.) 5 x 3⅛. Endorsed: "From his Fredericksburg, 1791."
10. Mercer, Hugh. Duplicate.
11. St. Clair, General Arthur. (1734-1818.) 5 x 4. Endorsed: "Gen'l Arthur St. Clair, New York, August, 1790."
12. Trumbull, Jonathan and his wife and daughter. India ink wash. 5 x 5.

Trumbull — *Continued:* 93

13. Trumbull, Mrs. Jonathan, mother of the artist. India ink wash. 5 x 3¾. Endorsed: "Mrs. (Faith) Trumbull, October, 1780. J. Trumbull, July, 1783."
14. Trumbull, Joseph. 5 x 3¾. Endorsed: "Jos. Trumbull, Esq., Obt., June, 1778. J. Trumbull, memoritor, July, 1783." Owned by Mr. Hall Parke McCullough, 1922.
15. Wythe, George. (1726-1806.) 3⅛ x 2⅞. Endorsed: "Geo. Wythe, 25th April, '91." Owned by Mr. Albert Rosenthal, Pa., 1922.
16. Unknown man supposed to be Major John André. 4½x3.
17. White, Brigadier General. Cardboard. 5 x 3⅛. Owned by Mr. Albert Rosenthal, Pa., 1922.

VALDENUIT

Flourished 1796-1797, New York.
Engraver.

He was the assistant of Saint-Mémin and some of the early portrait engravings bear his signature. Stauffer suggests that he may have merely been Saint-Mémin's pressman. Against this suggestion may be set the fact that the pressman is mentioned in Dexter's "Saint-Mémin"; also the fact that a few plates prior to 1797 bear the signature "St. Mémin and Valdenuit, No. 12 Fair St., N. York"; and also the entry listed below:

1. Van Cortlandt, Pierre. (1721-1814.) Pastel. Drawn 1797. Mentioned in R. Bolton: History of Westchester County, New York, 1848. Then at Cortlandt Manor, Croton River. See page 110.

VANDERLYN, John

b. *October, 1776, Kingston, New York;* d. *there 1852.*
Historical and portrait painter in oils and miniatures.

Valdenuit — Vanderlyn: 94

JOHN VANDERLYN was taken by his brother, Dr. Peter Vanderlyn to New York in 1792. In 1794 he was employed in a print store kept by a Mr. Barrow. During his leisure he studied at Robertson's Drawing Academy. He also copied several portraits by Gilbert Stuart and visited that painter in Philadelphia. Among the first to become a patron was Aaron Burr. He was in Europe during 1801-1815 and while he was in Paris he painted the celebrated nude "Ariadne." In Rome in 1807 he painted "Marius at Carthage" which received a gold medal upon its exhibition in Paris.

For several years he exhibited panoramas in New York, New Orleans and Havana. He returned to Paris in 1843-1844 with the commission to paint "The Landing of Columbus." The painting however he left to a French artist and the late C. H. Hart said that none of the work was done by Vanderlyn. He died in extreme poverty in his native town. An anonymous writer in "Putnam's Magazine" for June, 1854, gives some personal recollections of Vanderlyn. Tuckerman gives an extended account of Vanderlyn in his "Book of the Artists." See also "Atlantic Monthly," April, 1867 and "Art In America," February, 1917.

1. Barlow, Joel. (1754-1812.) Owned by Mr. P. T. Barlow, 1909. Reproduced in A. C. Sutcliffe: Robert Fulton, p. 171.
2. Church, Mrs. Edward and child. Crayon.
3. Church, Eliza Maria. Dated 1799. Crayon.
4. Church, Sarah Russell. Crayon.
5. Church, Edward. Crayon.

Vanderlyn — *Continued:* 95

6. Davie, William Richardson. "Engraved by J. B. Long-acre from a drawing by Mr. Vanderlyn taken in 1800."
7. Fulton, Robert. (1769-1815.) Drawn at 50 rue Vaugirard, Paris, the home of Joel Barlow from 1797-1804. Owned by Mr. P. T. Barlow. Reproduced in A. C. Sutcliffe: Robert Fulton, p. 115.
8. Gerry, Elbridge. (1744-1814.) Drawn 1798. Crayon. Owned by Miss Gerry, New Haven, 1892. Engraved by J. B. Longacre for National Portrait Gallery. Reproduced in "Magazine of American History, November, 1884; C. W. Bowen: Centennial, p. 92.
9. Irving, Washington. (1783-1859.) "Eng. by H. B. Hall after a drawing by Vanderlyn made in Paris in 1805," in Wilson: Bryant and his Friends.
10. Strobel, Mrs. Daniel. Crayon.
11. Jackson, Andrew. Drawn in pen and ink as a study for the head of his Jackson now in New York City Hall in the body of a letter to R. E. W. Earl the portrait painter, giving a description of his intended portrait of Jackson. Owned by Mr. Harry MacNeill Bland, N. Y., 1923.

VOLOZON, Denis A.

Flourished 1811-1820, Philadelphia.
Landscape painter and portrait draughtsman in crayons.

VOLOZON was a Frenchman who settled in Philadelphia, exhibited at the Academy and taught drawing there. He also made historical compositions.

1. Washington, George. Crayon. Pennsylvania Academy, 1812.

WELLMORE, E.

Flourished 1834-1839.
Engraver and miniature painter.

Pupil of Longacre. Worked both in Philadelphia and New York. It is said he went later into the ministry.

1. Mina the murderer. Lithographed by Child and Inman from an original drawing by E. Wellmore, made in his cell, 1832.

WENTWORTH

Flourished 1815, Utica, New York.
Portrait painter in oils and miniature.

He also made profile portraits in pencil.

WEST, BENJAMIN

b. *October 10, 1738, near Springfield, Chester County, Pennsylvania; d. March 11, 1820, London.*
Historical and portrait painter.

BENJAMIN WEST painted portraits in Philadelphia in 1756 and in New York in 1758. In 1760 he sailed for Rome and lived there until 1763 when he went to London where he spent the rest of his life. He instructed or assisted most of the American artists living in or passing through London. Peale, Pratt, Stuart, Trumbull, Brown, Wright, King and Malbone were some of the artists who were indebted to him either for his hospitality or instruction.

1. Franklin, Benjamin. (1706-1790.) Pen and ink outline in profile. Reproduced in Century Magazine, June, 1899, p. 301. Owned by Mr. S. W. Pennypacker, 1900.
2. Copley, Elizabeth and John S., Jr. Signed: "Benj. West, Master Copley, and his elder sister." Owned by Lord Averdare. Reproduced in Pelham Copley Papers, Mass. Hist. Collections, v. 71, 1914, p. 270.
3. Copley, Miss. Reproduced in 1610.

Wentworth — West, B.: 97

WEST, WILLIAM EDWARD

b. *December 10, 1788, Lexington, Kentucky;* d. *November 2, 1857, Nashville, Tennessee.*

Historical painter and portrait painter in oils and miniature.

WEST painted miniatures several years before he studied in Philadelphia with Thomas Sully about 1807. In 1819 he went to Nachez where he stayed until 1820 when he sailed for Europe. At Leghorn he painted a portrait of Byron. The pencil portrait he made of Shelly listed below was the basis for his oil painting and had the greater value in that it was taken from life. In 1824 he was in Paris. From 1825 to 1839 he was in London. The latter year he sailed for Baltimore. In 1840 he was in New York where he lived until 1855, when he moved to Nashville where he died. See: "Century Magazine," October, 1905; "Putnam's Magazine," September, 1907; and Tuckerman "Book of the Artists."

1. Shelly, Percy Bysshe. Pencil. Owned by Mrs. J. Dunn, 1905.

WILSON, MATTHEW

b. *July 17, 1814, London;* d. *February 23, 1892, Brooklyn, New York.*

Portrait painter in oils and miniature and crayon portrait draughtsman.

He was a pupil of Inman and first exhibited miniatures in Philadelphia. In 1835 he was in Paris. He was elected N. A. in 1843. From 1861 to 1893 he was a popular crayon and pastel portrait draughtsman in Hartford, Connecticut.

West, W. E.—Wilson: 98

WOOD, Joseph

b. *about 1778, Clarkstown, New York;* d. *1852, Washington, D. C.*
Portrait painter in oils and miniature.

Joseph Wood was the son of a farmer who was also the sheriff of Clarkstown, New York. The story is told that his father locked him up in the court house steeple because he neglected other work for drawing. Much against his father's wishes he walked to New York with only a few dollars in his pocket in 1793, intending to earn his living with his pencil. He wanted to become a landscape painter, but by chance his talents were directed to miniature painting. After several years doing odd work during the winters and playing the violin during the summers, he happened to see a miniature in a shop window and asked permission to copy it. This started him on his career. In 1804 he formed a partnership with John Wesley Jarvis, painting miniatures. Dunlap records a visit he made with Malbone to their studio during 1805-1806. Both artists received some assistance from Malbone at the time. The partnership was dissolved in 1809 and Wood had a studio at 160 Broadway during 1812-1813. The latter year he went to Philadelphia and had a studio at 93 South Third Street. His name occurs in the Philadelphia directories until 1817. He exhibited at the Academy. He moved later to Washington and in 1827 had a studio on the north side of Pennsylvania Avenue between 9th and 10th Sts. Pencil portraits by Joseph Wood are excellent. An ex-

Wood: 99

tended account of the artist appeared in "The Port-Folio," 1811.

1. Paulding, James Kirke. (1778-1860.) "Engraved by F. Halpin from a drawing by Joseph Wood," for Wilson: Bryant and his Friends, p. 127.

WUNDER, ADALBERT

b. *Berlin, Germany, February 5, 1807; d. after 1879. Portrait draughtsman in ink and crayon.*

He was in Hartford from 1855 to 1869. In 1879 he was in Hamilton, Ontario. He studied during 1843-1846 in Berlin and during 1846-1848 in Dresden.

Wunder: 99

INDEX

Akers, Charles
Alexander, Francis
Allen, Sarah Lockhart
Anderson, A.
Andre, John
Armstrong, William G.
Audubon, John James

Badger, John C.
Barry, Charles A.
Bensell, G. F.
Birch, B.
Birch, W.
Black, William Thurston
Blackburn, Joseph
Blyth, Benjamin
Boudier
Bowers, Edward
Browere, J. H. I.
Brown, "Mysterious"

Cheney, Seth Wells
Church, Frederick Edwin
Cole, Thomas
Collier, J. Howard
Colyer, Vincent
Cooper, Peregrine F.
Copley, John Singleton

Darley, William M. S.

Dubourjal, Savinien Edme
Duggan, Peter P.
Dunlap, William
Durand, Asher B.
Du Simitiere, P. E.
Duvivier

Fairman, Gideon
Ferris, Stephen, Jr.
Field, Robert
Fisher, J. J.
Florimont, Austin
Fraser, Charles
Fulton, Robert
Furnass, William H.

Gove, E. M.

Haines, William
Hall, H. B.
Hanley, W. H.
Hartwell, Alonso
Hazlitt, John
Herring, James
Hoffy, A.
Huntington, D.

Inman, Henry

Jackson, J. A.

Janvier, A. W.
Jarvis, John Wesley
Johnson, Eastman
Johnson, Henrietta
Johnston, David C.
Johnston, John
Johnston, Thomas M.
Judkins, E. M.

Kimberley, D.
Kosciuszko, Tadeusz A. B.

Lambdin, James R.
Lawrence, Samuel
Lawrie, Alexander, Jr.
Lemet, L.
Leslie, Eliza
Leslie, Charles R.
Longacre, James B.
Loud, Mrs. H. C.

Malbone, Edward Greene
Martin
Martin, Charles
Mason, G.
Masson, E.
Miles, Edward

Negus, Caroline
Newsam, A.
Newton, Gilbert Stuart

Peale, Charles Willson
Pease, J. I.
Perkins, Miss
Persico, Gennarino
Pine, R. E.

Quesnay, A. M.

Ramage, J.
Roberts, John
Robertson, Archibald
Ropes, Joseph
Rowse, Samuel W.
Saint-Mémin, C. B. J. F.

Savage, Edward
Schoener, J.
Sharples, Felix
Sharples, James
Sharples, Mrs. James
Sharples, James, Jr.
Shindler, A. Z.
Staigg, R. M.
Story, W. W.
Stuart, Gilbert
Sully, R. M.
Sully, Thomas

Thornton, William
Trumbull, John

Valdenuit
Vanderlyn, John
Volozon, Denis A.

Wellmore, E.
Wentworth
West, Benjamin
West, W. E.
Wilson, M.
Wood, Joseph
Wunder, A.

INDEX

Brown, H. K.—Cheney
Brown, Mrs.—Sharples
Brown, Mrs. G.—Copley
Brown, Mrs. H. K.—Cheney
Brown, Jacob—Suily
Brown, John—Sharples
Browne, A. M.—Sharples
Broughton, T.—Johnston
Bryant, W. C.—Cheney
Bull, O.—Darley
Bullard, L.—Rowse
Bullard, W. S.—Rowse
Burr, A.—Sharples, Saint-Mémin
Bush, Miss—Sharples

Cabell, H. H.—Saint-Mémin
Cabell, W. H.—Saint-Mémin
Cabot, G.—Copley
Cachasunghia—Saint Mémin
Calhoun, J. C.—Longacre
Campbell, J.—Saint-Mémin
Cannon, L.—Johnson
Carroll, C.—Longacre, Saint-
    Mémin
Cass, L.—Longacre
Chapman, N.—Longacre
Chardon, P.—Copley
Chase, S.—Longacre, Trumbull
Cheney, C.—Cheney
Cheney, Mrs. E. D.—Cheney
Cheney, Mrs. E. W.—Cheney
Cheney, J.—Rowse
Cheney, S. W.—Cheney,
    Kimberly
Cheney, Mrs. W.—Cheney
Cheney, W.—Cheney
Church, E.—Vanderlyn

Church, Mrs. E.—Vanderlyn
Church, E. M.—Vanderlyn
Church, S. R.—Vanderlyn
Clarke, J.—Cheney
Cleveland, W.—Saint-Mémin
Clinton, DeW.—Sharples
Clinton, G.—Saint-Mémin
Clinton, J.—Sharples
Clinton, Lady—Saint-Mémin
Coale, M. A.—Saint-Mémin
Cocke, J.—Saint-Mémin
Cogan, T.—Sharples
Cole, T.—Church
Cooke, G. F.—Leslie
Cooper, Miss—Copley
Cooper, S.—Copley
Copley, J. S.—Copley
Copley, Mrs. J. S.—Copley
Cox, Mrs.—Saint-Mémin
Crafts, Mrs. M. M.—Cheney
Cranch, C. P.—Story
Cranch, Mrs. C. P.—Darley
Cruger, H.—Sharples
Cunningham, Mrs. J. A.—
    Cheney
Curtis, B.—Rowse
Curtis, Mrs. C. P.—Cheney
Curtis, G. W.—Rowse
Curwen, S.—Blyth
Cushing, Mrs. W.—Sharples
Custis, E. P.—Sharples, Saint-
    Mémin
Custis, G. W. P.—Sharples

Dale, R.—Longacre
Darvin, E.—Sharples
Davie, W. R.—Vanderlyn

Davy, Sir H.—Sharples
Dayton, E.—Sharples
Deane, S.—Du Simitiere
Dearborn, J.—Du Simitiere
Decatur, S.—Saint-Mémin
De Lisle, H. C.—H. Johnson
De Lisle, Mlle.—H. Johnson
De Peyster, F.—E. Johnson
Dering, T.—Blackburn
Dickerson, John—Du Simitiere
Dix, D. L.—Cheney
Dobbin, J. C.—Johnson
Drayton, W. H.—Du Simitiere
Dumaresq, P.—Staigg
Dumaresq, Mrs. P.—Copley
Dunbar, Sir G.—Sharples
Durand, A. B.—Rowse
Dwight, Mrs. D.—Johnston
Dwight, H.—Rowse

Eaton, J. H.—Longacre
Eliot, J.—Copley
Ellery, W.—Trumbull
Emerson, G. S.—Cheney
Emerson, R. W.—Rowse,
    Johnson
Everett, M.—Copley

Felton, C. C.—E. Johnson
Few, W.—Sharples
Field, J. T.—Rowse
Field, K.—Rowse
Fisher, M.—Sharples
Flagg, S.—J. Johnston
Fox, K.—Cheney
Franklin, B.—B. West
Frothingham, Mrs. S.—Cheney

Fulton, R.—Vanderlyn, Fulton

Gaines, E. P.—Sully
Gale, C.—H. Johnson
Gallatin, A.—Sharples
Gallego, Mr.—Field
Gamble, R.—Saint-Mémin
Gannett, E. S.—Rowse
Gardiner, G. A.—Cheney
Garet, P.—Johnson
Gates, H.—Sharples, Trumbull,
    Du Simitiere
Gay, E.—Hazlitt
Gerry, E.—Vanderlyn
Gibaut, J.—Blyth
Gibbes, Mrs. J.—H. Johnson
Giles, A.—Saint-Mémin
Giles, Mrs. A.—Saint-Mémin
Glover, Gen.—Trumbull
Goddard, Mrs. C. A.—Cheney
Goddard, Mrs. F. N.—Johnson
Godwin, G.—Sharples
Godwin, J.—Sharples
Godwin, S. W.—Sharples
Godwin, W.—Sharples
Goodman, Mrs. R.—Cheney
Goodman, R. C.—Cheney
Gore, C.—Copley
Gourdin, T.—Saint-Mémin
Grant, E. W.—Cheney
Gray, A.—Cheney
Greaves, R.—Sharples
Green, A.—Sharples
Green, Mrs. E.—Copley
Green, F.—Sharples
Green, J.—Copley
Green, M. G.—Sharples

Greenleaf, Nancy—Cranch
Greene, J.—Copley
Greene, Mrs. J.—Copley
Greene, N.—Trumbull
Griffith, Mrs. R. E.—Sharples

H., H. W.—Cheney
Hall, H.—Copley
Halleck, F. G.—Inman
Hamilton, A.—Sharples, Saint-
  Mémin, Fairman
Hamilton, Mrs. A.—Martin,
  Johnson
Hammond, S.—Cheney
Hammond, Mrs. S. G.—Cheney
Hancock, J.—Trumbull
Hancock, T.—Copley
Hancock, Mrs. T.—Copley
Harper, R. G.—Saint-Mémin
Harrison, B.—Johnson
Hastings, S.—Saint-Mémin
Hawthorne, N.—Rowse, Johnson
Haygarth, Dr.—Sharples
Hayne, R. Y.—Longacre
Hazard, E. and Mrs. E.—
  Duvivier
Henshaw, S.—Copley
Herbert, R. B.—Saint-Mémin
Herschel, A.—Sharples
Higginson,—Cheney
Higginson, C. P.—Rowse
Higginson, T. W.—Johnson
Hill, H.—Copley
Hill, Mrs. H.—Copley
Hill, R.—Sharples
Hill, W.—Saint-Mémin
Hoar, E.—Hartwell

Hobart, J. S.—Sharples
Hoffman, C. F.—Inman
Hoffman, S. P.—Johnson
Holthrop, Mrs.—Johnson
Holyoke, E.—Blyth, Copley
Hooper, Mrs. A.—Cheney
Hopkins, J.—Trumbull
Hopkins, S.—Trumbull
Howard, J. E.—Trumbull
Howes, Mrs. F.—Cheney
Howes, L. C.—Cheney
Hunt, E. L.—Cheney
Huntington, F. D.—Cheney
Huntington, Mrs. F. D.—Cheney
Huntington, S.—Du Simitiere
Hutchinson, T.—Copley

Indians, Eight portraits of—
  Saint-Mémin
Ingersoll, J.—Sharples
Inman, H.—Inman
Irving, W.—Vanderlyn, Jarvis
Israel, Mrs. I.—Sharples

Jackson, A.—Longacre, Sully
Jackson, C. T.—Cheney
Jackson, F. J.—Sharples
Jackson, Mrs. F. J.—Sharples
Jackson, J.—Copley
Jackson, J.—Longacre
Jackson, J.—Cheney
Jackson, Mrs. J.—Cheney
Jay, J.—Du Simitiere
Jefferson, T.—Longacre, Saint-
  Mémin, Sharples, Stuart,
  Thornton, Kosciuszko
Jenkins, Mrs. L.—Copley

Jenkins, N.—E. Johnson
Johnson, Dr.—Sharples
Johnson, E.—E. Johnson
Johnson, W. S.—Sharples
Johnston, J.—J. Johnston
Johnston, Lady—Saint-Mémin

Kennedy, J. P.—E. Johnson
Kennedy, R. L.—E. Johnson
Kent, J.—Sharples
King, J.—Sharples

Lafayette, M. J. P. R. Y. G. M.—
   Audubon, Sharples
Lang, Mrs. W. B.—Cheney
Langdon, J.—Sharples
La Roche Fancould—Sharples
Latimer, J.—Saint-Mémin
Laurens, H.—Armstrong, Du
   Simitiere, Sharples
Law, T.—Sharples
Lawrence, Mrs. A. A.—Cheney
Le Fevre—Sharples
Lee, S.—Saint-Mémin
Lee, Mrs. S.—Saint-Mémin
Leslie, Mrs. S. L.—Cheney
Lincoln, A.—E. Johnson
Liotard, J. E.—Copley
Liston, Sir R.—Sharples
Liston, Lady—Sharples
Littlehale, H. P.—Cheney
Livermore, S.—Sharples
Livingston, E.—Longacre
Livingston, R. R.—Sharples
Longfellow, H. W.—Alexander,
   Rowse, Lawrence, Cheney,
   Johnson

Longfellow, Mrs. H. W.—Rowse
Longfellow, S.—E. Johnson
Longfellow, Mrs. S.—E. Johnson
Loring, A.—Cheney
Loring, C. G.—Cheney
Loring, C. W.—Cheney
Loring, F. C.—Cheney
Loring, J. L.—Cheney
Lottmer, Col.—Johnson
Louvilliere, J.—Perisco
Lowell, A. C.—Cheney
Lowell, A.—Cheney
Lowell, E.—Cheney
Lowell, F. C.—Rowse
Lowell, Mrs. F. D.—Rowse
Lowell, J. R.—Rowse, Cheney
Lyman, A. T.—Cheney
Lyman, Mrs. C. T.—Cheney

Macomb, A.—Saint-Mémin,
   Sully
MacHenry, J.—Saint-Mémin,
   Sharples
Madison, J.—Longacre, Sharples
Madison, Mrs. J.—Sharples,
   Herring, Johnson
Mann, Mrs. L.—Cheney
Manning, D.—Johnson
Marion, F.—Longacre
Marshall, J.—Saint-Mémin
Martin, A.—Sharples
Mason, E. R.—Cheney
Mason, J.—Sharples
Mason, Jane—Cheney
Mason, T.—Sharples
May, E.—Furnass
May, Mrs. M.—Cheney

Mayhew, J.—Copley
Mazyck, Mrs. P.—H. Johnston
McClurg, J.—Sharples
McCosh, Mrs. J.—Johnson
McKean, T.—Sharples
Mercer, H.—Trumbull
Merrow, Mrs.—Cheney
Miles, N. A.—Johnson
Miller, J.—Sully
Mills, A. C. L. D.—Cheney
Mills, C. J.—Cheney
Mitchell, S. L.—Sharples
Monroe, J.—Sharples
Montpensier, Duke—Sharples
Moore, C. C.—Sharples
Morgan, D.—Herring
Morgan, Mrs.—Sharples
Morison, J. H.—Cheney
Morris, G.—Sharples
Morris, G. P.—Inman
Morris, R.—Du Simitiere
Morris, S.—Saint-Mémin
Morse, Mrs. H.—Cheney
Morse, J.—Sharples
Munson, Judge—E. Johnson
Murdock, Mr. J.—Cheney
Murray, J.—Copley
Murray, M.—Saint-Mémin
Myrick, Captain—E. Johnson

Nash, S. P.—Johnson
Newton, G. S.—Newton
Nicholas, P. N.—Saint-Mémin
Nicholson, Mrs. L.—Sharples
North, W.—Sharples
Norton, C. E.—Rowse
Norton, Mrs. C. E.—Rowse

Norton, G.—Rowse
Norton, J.—Rowse
Norton, S.—Rowse

Page, S. D.—Du Simitiere
Paine, R. T.—Savage, Longacre
Parker, J.—Saint-Mémin
Parker, T.—Cheney
Parker, Mrs. T.—Cheney
Parkman, S.—Cheney
Parramore, Mrs. T.—Sharples
Patterson, J.—Sharples
Patterson, Mrs. J.—Sharples
Paulding, J. K.—Wood
Paulding, W.—Durand
Payouska—Saint-Mémin
Peabody, C.—Cheney
Peabody, E.—Cheney
Pekenino, M.—Durand
Pelham, H.—Copley
Pepoon, Mr.—Johnson
Pepperell, W.—Copley
Perkins, C. C.—Cheney
Perkins, J. H.—Cheney
Perkins, T. H. 2d—Cheney
Perkins, Mrs. T. H. 2d—Cheney
Perkins, Mrs. T. H. 3d—Cheney
Persico, L.—E. Johnson
Peters, R.—E. Johnson
Philippe, Louis—Sharples
Phillips, M. W.—Copley
Pickering, T.—Longacre
Pierce, Mrs.—Johnson
Pierce, M.—Cheney
Pinckney, C. C.—Sharples
Pitkin, A.—Cheney
Pitkin, E.—Cheney

Poinsett, J. R.—Longacre
Porter, D.—Sully
Porter, W. T.—Inman
Powell, J.—Copley
Powell, Mrs. J.—Copley
Pratt, M.—Cheney
Priestley, J.—Sharples
Prioleau, E.—H. Johnson
Prioleau, Mrs. E.—H. Johnson
Putnam, C. and A. E.—Cheney
Putnam, E. C.—Cheney
Putnam, G.—Cheney
Putnam, Mrs. G.—Cheney
Putnam, I.—Trumbull
Putnam, Mrs. G. and C.—
    Cheney
Putnam, J. L.—Rowse
Putnam, Mrs. J. P.—Cheney
Putnam, R.—Sharples

Ramsey, D.—Fraser
Ravenel, Mrs. D.—Johnston
Ravenel, Mrs. R. L.—Johnston
Read, T. B.—Lawrie
Reed, J.—Du Simitiere
Revere, P.—Saint-Mémin
Rider, A.—Saint-Mémin
Ripley, J.—Sully
Ripley, Mrs.—Cheney
Robertson, T. B.—Saint-Mémin
Robinson, Miss—Sharples
Ross, M.—Fulton
Royall, P.—Copley
Rush, B.—Sharples, Haines
Russell, S. H.—Cheney
Rutledge, E.—Longacre
Rutledge, J.—Herring

Rutter, M.—Longacre

Sales, F.—Judkins
Sanderson, B.—Cheney
Sargent, T.—Longacre
Scott, W.—Sully
Seaver, Miss—Cheney
Sedgwick, C. M.—Cheney
Sedgwick, T.—Saint-Mémin
Shaw, L.—Rowse
Shaw, M.—Rowse
Shaw, P.—Rowse
Shaw, Mrs. P. A.—Rowse
Shaw, Q.—Rowse
Shaw, R.—Rowse
Shelly, P. B.—W. E. West
Sherbourne, H.—Sharples
Shippen, E.—André
Simmons, Mrs. W.—Cheney
Skyrin, J.—Sharples
Small, J.—Copley
Smith, Alex.—Saint-Mémin
Smith, Armistead—Sharples
Smith, Edna D.—Cheney
Smith, Elihu—Sharples
Smith, Isaac—Sharples
Smith, J. A.—Saint-Mémin
Smith, Louis—Saint-Mémin
Smith, M. T.—Sharples
Smith, Reuben—Sharples
Smith, Samuel—Sharples, Saint-
    Mémin
Smith, William—Copley
Smith, Mrs. William—Cheney
Smith, William L.—Sharples
Smith, William P.—Sharples
Southey, R.—Sharples

Spaight, R. D.—Saint-Mémin, Sharples
Sparks, M. C.—Rowse
Spencer, O. M.—Longacre
Sprague, Mrs. F. G.—Cheney
Standard, J.—Saint-Mémin
Steuben, F. von—Du Simitiere
Stewart, C.—Sully
Stewart, J.—Sharples
St. Clair, A.—Trumbull, Longacre
Stillman, S.—Doyle
Stillman, W. J.—Rowse
Stoddard, R. H.—Lawrie
Stone, E.—Blyth
Storer, E.—Copley
Storer, Mrs. E.—Copley
Story, J.—Story
Stoughton, W.—Sharples
Strobel, Mrs. D.—Vanderlyn
Strutt, W—Sharples
Stuart, G.—Stuart
Sturges, H. K.—Rowse
Sully, J. C.—Sully
Sully, S. and J.—Sully
Sully, T.—Lawrie, Sully
Sumner, C.—Johnson
Sumpter, T.—Armstrong
Swartout, S.—Saint-Mémin
Symmes, J. C.—Audubon

Tallmadge, B.—Trumbull
Tallyrand—Sharples
Taylor, C.—Saint-Mémin
Taylor, Mrs. C.—Saint-Mémin
Taylor, Mrs. R.—Johnston
Temple, B.—Sharples

Temple, Mrs. B.—Sharples
Temple, J.—Sharples, Copley
Temple, Lady—Sharples, Copley
Thomas, Isiah—Sharples
Thomas, Gen.—Blyth
Thoreau, H. D.—Rowse
Thouisy, de—Sharples
Ticknor, Mrs. G.—Cheney
Todd, S. V.—Sharples
Tompkins, Mrs. C.—Sharples
Townsend, C.—Sharples
Traille, R.—Copley
Tredell, J.—Saint-Mémin
Trumbull, Jos.—Trumbull
Trumbull, Mrs. J.—Trumbull
Trumbull, J. and wife—Trumbull
Tucker, T. T.—Saint-Mémin
Turner, W.—Copley
Twisleton, Mrs. E.—Cheney
Tyler, J.—Copley
Tyler, John—Lambdin

Van Berckel—Sharples
Van Buren, M.—Longacre
Van Cortlandt, P.—Sharples
Vanderhorst, Mr.—Sharples
Van Horne, J.—Dunlap
Van Horne, Mrs. J.—Dunlap

Wadsworth, J.—Sharples
Ward, R.—Copley
Wales, M. A.—Cheney
Warren, E.—Cheney
Washington, G.—Saint-Mémin, Sharples, Volozon, Dunlap, Blyth, Peale, Du Simitiere, Ramage, Mr. S. Sharples